HOW TO GET PEOPLE TO GIVE YOU MONEY

By Asking the Right Questions

RICK OTTON

Disclaimer

Although the publisher and the author have made every effort to ensure that the information in this book was correct at press time and while this publication is designed to provide accurate information in regard to the subject matter covered, the publisher and the author assume no responsibility for errors, inaccuracies, omissions, or any other inconsistencies herein and hereby disclaim any liability to any party for any loss, damage, or disruption caused by errors or omissions, whether such errors or omissions result from negligence, accident, or any other cause.

This publication is meant as a source of valuable information for the reader, however it is not meant as a substitute for direct expert assistance. If such level of assistance is required, the services of a competent professional should be sought.

The publisher and the author do not make any guarantee or other promise as to any results that may be obtained from using the content of this book. The author is not a professional certificated in any medical or neighboring disciplines and provides examples in this book from his own experience. The results achieved by others may not be typical.

The publisher and the author are providing this book and its contents on an "as is" basis. Your use of the information in this book is at your own risk.

www.theupgradedthinking.com

How To Get People To Give You Money

ASK ME HOW I KNOW

Imagine waking up to find you've lost your job and your cash savings will only last a few weeks.

Imagine your successful business has just collapsed overnight and you can't pay your employees.

Imagine being unable to liquidate any assets in order to survive.

Imagine access to all your bank accounts frozen.

Imagine access to your pension fund, superannuation fund or 401(k) taken by the Government.

Imagine all this came about through marketing my real estate teachings and a book that set out to help people, but which instead resulted in a Federal Court action ending with a fine of $18m.

Well, my guess is that you may not need much imagination if you're reading this now, in the midst of an unprecedented crisis that has hit the entire planet. The impact of COVID-19 on your life, your family, your health, your income, your future, will last years, if not decades. And this is only the start of a long and tough recovery period. Sadly, not everyone will make it through the other end.

Right now, no one knows what will happen in the future, short term or long term. Speaking from experience, the emotional roller coaster of *not knowing* is more fundamental and causes us more anxiety and stress than the mere loss of success or money. I never envisioned that one day I'd be sharing my hard learned lessons with you and so many others.

My name is Rick Otton and I've lived through all of the above scenarios, but mine happened before the arrival of COVID-19. I had to learn the hard way how to put my life back together again. It occurred to me that the ways we recover and rebuild our lives don't really change. So I set out to write this book to help you reset, rebuild and become more resilient to get through this current crisis.

So what makes me qualified to help *you*?

On 18th November 2018, a Federal Court made a judgment against me that included a massive fine. It was extremely demoralizing, thoroughly depressing and during my lowest points, I did consider ending it all. The reason I mention this is because it's important to 'own' our mistakes.

It would be wrong of me in writing this introduction not to mention that this Federal Court case existed and to acknowledge that I was at fault. Today, as I move on with my life, I freely admit that the judgment was the correct one. We all make mistakes in life - the most important thing is to recognize them as being part of life and keep moving forward.

When I was born, my mother told everyone I was *spastic* — a word no one uses today but which unfortunately was common back then. She used to tell me over and over again that the doctors had given up on me - until one day a doctor came up with an idea for reducing water or pressure on my brain (I don't remember which!). Anyway, he fixed me, but I ended up with a unique logic system that finds unusual ways to solve problems. As I grew up, I realized that what was simple logic to me was big news to most other people. And that encouraged me to try to help others to see things the way I do.

I share this with you to give context to my story. In the late 80s and 90s I found myself buying repossessed real estate from failed financial institutions in the southern states of the US - not because I particularly liked real estate, but because I had developed ways to earn money from it that did not require large amounts of capital. I also loved the idea of making properties available to people who were struggling to get finance during those tough times.

By the late 90s, friends started telling me about the problems facing homebuyers back home and asked if I could adapt my system for other countries using English Law.

After a few years, numerous legal meetings and much creative thinking, I came up with *the new standard*, a simpler and easier way that would help buyers and sellers move in and out of home ownership, rather than the *standard* way that everyone felt was broken. I saw real estate as helping others solve a problem which just happened to involve real estate.

It worked really well. I had no marketing budget, however the fact that I was helping people who wanted a simpler way to buy and sell real estate meant I always had people asking for my help. The business grew rapidly through positive media and word of mouth. And the turn on for me was the constant rush of dopamine to my brain as my exciting vision became reality.

Now as I look back on where I went wrong, it's clear that the company grew too fast. This meant that the real connections that mattered got lost over time, along with my original vision. And if I'm honest, I became less passionate and less connected with the helping side of things. Coupled with other poor business decisions, I drove my business over a cliff with my foot flat out on the accelerator. My income plummeted from somewhat high to so low that I was practically living on cheese from a mousetrap. And I discovered who my real friends and business associates were. Now I can see the court judgment and fine may have been a blessing in disguise that allowed me to press the *reset* button on my life.

With the COVID-19 crisis leaving so many people's lives and livelihoods shattered, I wanted to give back by sharing some of the tools I've used to help rebuild my own life so that you can use them too.

What this book will teach you

So I had to reset and rebuild my life. I broke down the key lessons that I learned from going wrong in order to move forwards and start to recover. It took a long time, but it was worth it. Now I'm definitely a little older and hopefully a little wiser. And I can share my experience and knowledge with you so that you too can reset and rebuild your life.

1/ Do what you love. Money results from that, not because of it

2/ Learn to pivot and adjust. Yesterday's thinking won't solve today's new problems

3/ Things don't change - people change things

One of the most interesting things that came out of my personal 'crash' - and which my gut tells me you'll also experience during this crisis, if you haven't already - is that my perspective of what I want from life has fundamentally changed. What I thought I wanted out of life - money, fame, fortune, material things - aren't what I now want. You know that expression, every cloud has a silver lining? That's so true. You just need to make sure you're carrying your own umbrella the next time it rains.

The standard way of thinking and doing things isn't the solution to survival when life throws you a curveball. And we can't model the future based on the past. No one can, but incredibly almost all experts refer to the past as their reasoning for us to do x or y. But right now, I think we can all see that the past has not prepared us for the *future* — which has just become the *present*. Events that normally take years to happen have occurred in a matter of just weeks.

If we consider the old ways of doing things, many of us are already realising that they're no longer fit for purpose. I like to think of them as blunt instruments, like a *sledgehammer*. If we can, it's much better to fix things using a *screwdriver* that has maximum impact with minimum side effects.

We need to ask ourselves, 'Is where I am now where I want to be?'. We're facing a unique opportunity to restore, but on our own terms, not somebody else's.

When we communicate with each other we use a lot of 'short hand' to say what we really mean, and the tone and sound of how we say things is incredibly important. Because words are often flat on the pages of a book I've included a link to audio at the end of this book where you can hear me using scripts in real world situations and show you how to 'hack' the embedded scripts that we all use every day to get the results you want.

In this book I'll show you all the tools I used for my personal recovery that you can adapt to any situation you find yourself in. I'll give you some real life examples and scripts that you can use in different scenarios. Whether it's asking your landlord to delay or reduce your rental payments, asking your bank to relax your overdraft rules, convincing your boss to keep you on, or coping in another lockdown with your family.

So are you ready to reset and rebuild your life? It won't be an easy journey, but ask yourself, do you really have a choice?

The Deck Reshuffles

If you could wind back your life, are there things you'd do differently?

Well, the silver lining in this cloud may be that we've all been given a *wind back* opportunity to do things differently -- because the deck just got reshuffled for the majority of the planet's population.

To put it another way, it's how we play this second half. We can either see the road ahead as utter chaos or we can see it as a golden opportunity. But, as someone who has already had to reconstruct his life, I discovered that simply seeing the opportunity without putting the best structure in place will result in chaos. So to play this second half, the thrill will not be searching for the light at the end of the tunnel but *striving to be the driver of your very own train*. In my own situation, the bounce back only began after I was able to make one fundamental shift in thinking that was life changing.

We're all in the self-esteem business. If we feel good

about who we are, what we do and how we do it, then we can end life with our parting words being - *Wow, that was so much fun!*

This book is a survival manual containing all the tools that I've used to reset and restore life back from my personal 'crash'.

Some people take cocaine for the dopamine release, which seems to me a rather expensive way to feel good. But when we have a vision to follow, then the passion to fulfil it will create the same rush without having to resort to powder substances.

After coming through the 2008 financial crash and helping thousands of people rebuild their lives, I feel I've just watched the Titanic hit the iceberg full on, but this time I'm going to try to pull as many of you as possible into my lifeboat. You and me are in this boat together - it's just that what put us in it is different and we don't have a lot of time.

The ability to move forwards isn't because of what's in your wallet -- as I've realized this can easily be taken away -- but what's going on in your head and the ability to clearly see the road ahead, coupled with the available time you have left to act.

For the last few years I was able to survive by recreating and reinventing myself. But to do that I had to reconstruct my life. And to do that I needed to *communicate* in order to bring others on board to help me. I couldn't have done it all myself. We're all going to need help, but it's *how we ask for that help* that will be so crucial to the final result.

I know that I have an ability to communicate an idea in such a way that people like to join in or be a part of the result. I'm hoping that I can pass as much of that onto you as possible.

Today governments around the world are telling us to communicate with our landlord, bank, insurance company or employer in order to restructure our situation, except they don't tell us exactly how we're supposed to do that.

Do we write? Do we email? Do we call? And how do we structure sentences in order to achieve our desired outcome from our landlord, bank, insurance company or employer?

If for no other reason than selfishly allowing me to rewind my own past - allow me now to help you with everything you need to know, including the very *scripts* and *language patterns* that I use to communicate an idea from beginning to end.

Right now, these may appear to be just words on a page. However, towards the end of this book you'll find that I've laid out for you exactly what to do and say - based on a lifetime of study, experience and structured thinking.

I want you to be in the unique position where you can communicate with another person's *subconscious* mind, knowing how certain feelings, images and ideas will influence their thinking and in turn transmit those *'instructions'* to their *conscious* mind - resulting in people wanting to give you what you want while loving you at the same time.

Whereas most people communicate with another person's conscious mind, I've always found you get better results if you go straight to the boss - the subconscious mind - and let it pass the instructions down through to its underling, the conscious mind.

When we understand how people function, we can take

more control of the situations in which we find ourselves. By becoming successful at this, we become more successful in daily life. And by becoming successful in daily life, we develop immense self-esteem and self-confidence which is so paramount, particularly during a crisis.

This is a crisis to which I'm also party. I just arrived early and did some of the heavy lifting so you don't have to.

In this book you'll also meet my good friends the Mumbles. Barry, Betty and Little Chris Mumbles are a typical family you'd find anywhere in the world. They just happen to be the perfect example to help you understand the patterns of communication and interaction that we need. And they also look good in cartoons!

THE MUMBLES FAMILY

As I finish writing this introduction, the world is going through the most monumental changes since the Second World War. I realized after my personal 'crash' that we all need to reconnect with the tools with which we were born, in order to make sense of the changing world. If any of this helps you to make it through what's coming, then the turmoil that I went through will have been worthwhile.

Once again, what strange times we're living through.

Stay safe.

Rick

ONE

Once Upon A Time

YOU CAN'T DESCRIBE 'WET' UNLESS YOU'VE BEEN IN
THE POOL

We humans in the 21st century are in need of an instruction manual.

If we look at how we now communicate, compared to how we did thirty or forty years ago, it's radically different. Most of us communicate using technology, while the actual art of face to face interaction has kind of gone.

When you go on YouTube, there are countless dating and relationship coaches who teach things like '*5 things to say to a woman when you first meet*', '*What not to say to a boy on your first date*' or '*10 subjects never to talk to men about*' — really basic information. Ten or fifteen years ago we didn't need so much coaching because we did all our social learning while hanging out with other kids after school.

This issue of communicating to meet members of the opposite sex is just the tip of the iceberg. With the world in crisis, it's never been more important for us to be able to communicate clearly and quickly to other people in our lives.

To understand how we arrived at the smartphone age of isolated kids, we have to go back to the 70s or even before that. We kids would come home after school and Mom would say, '*Go and play with your friends. I'll call you in for dinner at six o'clock.*'

So what we all did was hang around the neighborhood with friends whose moms had said the same thing to them, and we'd play games like tag or hide and seek. We'd agree or disagree on things, such as who could play, who was '*it*', who was on which team. And we'd do this almost every day until Mom would call us at six o'clock.

This meant that we were constantly relating to other people and learning how to communicate. We would learn what they liked, what they tolerated and especially what annoyed them. What made them laugh, cry, or feel anxious. The result is that most of us approached new situations and social arenas like high school, college or first jobs with social skills we'd been learning since we were youngsters.

And these just became part of our communication *tool sets*. So by the time we reached drinking age and were about to meet a girl or a boy, we had an understanding of how the conversation was going to flow. And we were comfortable with it because we'd been relating to other people all our lives, right?

By the 80s however, people started moving away from houses and backyards into apartments and condominiums, and the old ways of playing and communicating began to disappear. The next best thing we had was the public park. Then our parents became more aware of the 'stranger danger' that sometimes lurked in parks and stories of bad things happening to kids became more mainstream. You'd see drugs turning up and moms would worry if their kids were hanging out there, especially after dark.

So technology began to take over in the way parents related to their kids. If Little Chris was at home upstairs playing on the Atari, then he couldn't get into trouble with the big kids in the park. But as a result, this changed the way that kids interacted with each other.

As the years went by, the appeal of computers, PlayStations and so on became the new normal. Now, going out after school and hanging out with your friends on the street corner is considered *child neglect*. The new normal became keeping kids indoors, away from threat and danger.

So once we started playing with technology instead of hanging out on the street corner or local park, we were no longer meeting in real time. Even in more recent times, for example with interconnected gaming consoles when Little Chris can play Super Mario The Comeback with fifty other kids worldwide, it's still not the same as when kids learned to play together face to face.

YESTERDAY **TODAY**

So let's take this further back.

Once upon a time if you wanted to communicate with

someone who was somewhere else, you'd write them a letter. You'd stick the letter in an envelope, buy a stamp and put it in the post box.

Then perhaps a week or so later if you were lucky you'd get a reply. Of course we had phones as well, but the phone was usually in a fixed place in the house. If you wanted to chat you'd sit on the bottom stair in the chilly hallway with the phone firmly fixed to the wall socket by a cable that was never long enough. For a while we also had fax machines, but most people still hand wrote 'letters' and then faxed them.

Then came email, replacing the letter and even the landline conversation. In the early days of email you could tell a person's age from their style of writing. Older people composed an email like a standard letter, all *pleases* and *thank yous*. On the other hand, younger people would sometimes just write a single line. No hellos, thanks or goodbyes. And all the kids learned how to use email and created a new standard in communicating. Then came SMS and they learned how to text, using shortcuts like 'Gr8' or 'c u later'.

 This behaviour change extended even to nightclubs. I recently went to a club in Ibiza where there were thousands of people. But it wasn't thousands of people listening to music, dancing and talking like they did 30 or 40 years ago. It was just loud music and everybody had a smartphone in their hand, communicating even with the person next to them, asking:

'What do u think of the music?'
'Yeah, gr8!,'

But there's no human interaction.

Hey, let's all meet up for a chat?

One of the side effects of all this is that the lack of social interaction skills can lead to binge drinking.

Let's imagine one day Little Chris is out with his buddies for the first time as an adult. They're in a night-club and he likes a girl by the bar. Once upon a time that would have been a simple interaction for those who grew up before the isolation effects of technology.

Little Chris thinks: 'I've been online, I've been trolling, I've looked at porn on my phone. But for the first time I've got to talk to a girl and I'm feeling very uncomfortable.'

As a result, Chris is incredibly anxious.

'But I've got to do something, or I'll end up a single old man.'

So what we do is find some Dutch courage, we say we'd better get some alcohol. In actual fact, we'd better get it down really, really fast.

'Because in a minute, I'm gonna have to chat to this girl and I don't know what to say to her.'

The result is an increase in binge drinking, as the way to communicate is often reduced to getting smashed on alcohol, simply to find the courage to say hello.

We have a world full of people who can't talk to each other, can't understand each other, can't sell to each other. Although everybody is speaking and using words, they're not necessarily the *right* ones.

Perhaps 30 years ago, people would understand why *she said that*, or why *he did that* or why people think what people think. These days, because we haven't grown up with these basic human interactions, when people say things or do things we don't understand, we're kinda lost.

We think, 'Oh, well, I don't *get* it.'

And when we don't get it, we can't understand it. And when we don't understand it, we *disconnect*.

The understanding of this disconnection is important.

We humans as a species were not designed to live in isolation. We function and perform better with continuous human interaction. If we look at the five 'Blue Zones' around the world, you'll see that the people who live the longest and healthiest rely heavily on social and communal interaction. This is why lockdown during COVID-19 has been so bad for our mental wellbeing.

Relanguage to Reposition

WORDS THAT WORK

If I ask someone today, *'How did you learn to communicate?'*—the answer will usually be 'on the job' or maybe a self help book. And that's usually only those who work in sales or marketing. If your world experience doesn't involve much of that, you may find that your experiences come mostly from school, college, workplace or friends.

30 or 40 years ago, life insurance companies invested a lot of money in their sales and marketing departments in order to teach *communication* skills, based on what was then cutting edge science on human behavior.

Human behavior scientists were even getting their research funded by the life insurance industry. At the time it was hugely profitable, with bottomless budgets for research and training. They used the latest information to teach their sales and marketing people how to sell, how to market and, most importantly, how to successfully communicate and interact with others.

That entire industry worldwide would have something like small universities for training on the same level as IBM. In fact, it was originally IBM that set up universities training these people alongside door to door sales companies. However, life insurance companies don't have the resources for sales teams anymore. The corporate budgets for this are gone and so too are these universities. Now nobody gets trained, nobody gets taught.

 Today we might see the giant campuses of Google or Microsoft but they're like closed worlds for tech workers rather than training for human interaction. Today, the majority of workers at these big tech companies are actually training machines to eventually take over and do their jobs.

And if you actually say to a 23 year old today, *'Here's a rate book and a laptop, go and sell something to somebody'* — whether it's a product or an idea or a concept — they have no idea how to communicate, because they haven't communicated with others in everyday life, except perhaps over alcohol.

So the only thing they can actually do is try to find books on persuasion techniques, negotiation, marketing, sales, and do the best they can to learn how to communicate.

Most books are written to show us how to persuade the *conscious* mind. But we will see that the *conscious* mind actually receives its instructions from its big brother — the *subconscious* mind. I could go to KFC and beg all day long for a Big Mac and it doesn't matter how persuasive I am, I'm still knocking on the wrong door. Instead, we need to be knocking on the *right* door and create an environment where they want to throw in the fries and drink for free.

I can love you or hate you in less than 90 seconds

But some of the rules of human behaviour haven't changed. For instance, when you meet someone for the first time they'll decide what they think about you within the first 90 seconds, and like the saying goes *'you never get a second chance to make a first impression'*. So if you're aware of this in a real situation, you'll know how to influence it rather than become a victim of it.

First impressions count. There's another expression, *you can't judge a book by its cover.* Well, that's kind of true but only when people have time to give you the benefit of the doubt and eventually get to know you.

But these days very few people are willing to take the long slow road of getting to know other people. Our attention spans are super limited. Think of how dating apps like Tinder work, swiping away a potentially amazing human connection in a matter of milliseconds.

With self confidence comes the ability to control events around you through improved communication. And when you can control events around you, the decisions you make on a daily basis will be more effective. More effective means getting to the punchline faster. More success with others. More success with others means more personal success.

Here's another example of how ridiculous things can get when we no longer have human interaction. A few years ago I decided to test my staff's alertness at my office.

I would go around the corner, secretly call the office then observe as they watched the phone ring. Even though they could see it was me, rather than pick up, they would send a text asking, 'Hey, Rick, did you try to call? I missed the phone, was it important?'

We tend not to answer a call these days, but usually let it go to voicemail. Then we can decide if we even want to call back. Some forward thinking companies moved their customer service to live chat. No one enjoys waiting on the customer service phone line for 27 minutes while listening to jingles. When it's live chat we can carry on texting and emailing while the customer service person is doing their thing.

These are subtle shifts in what we expect from communication with others. And then we're confused when dealing with friends, family, lovers and colleagues. We find it hard to read the signals and understand the subtle messages we're being constantly given.

Once our phones could only be found in our homes and were 100% all about talking to each other. Now the amount of audio communication for which people use their smart phones is down exponentially. If you'd said to somebody 10 years ago, you'll only ever make calls with your phone 23% of the time, while spending the rest of the time messaging, scrolling, watching or listening to content, people would have disagreed and told you how much they love to speak to their friends. And now they'll still say '*but I love speaking to my friends!*' It's just that now 'speak to my friends' means messaging.

Because we lack human communication we no longer feel comfortable speaking to people.

. . .

Why is it when someone tells me they're '99% sure we'll make this deal', then 100% of the time the deal never happens... even though they were '99% sure'?

- *What's that all about?*
- *How does that work?*

With the huge gaps in communication within our social and business environments, many of us don't have the required skill sets anymore. We need to teach ourselves to recognize visual and aural inputs, smell, words, body language, personal territories and zones.

We need to understand how all of these come together and how they affect what someone's feeling and how they're behaving. And here's why ...

With the world facing unprecedented challenges — probably the greatest since WW2 — everything in life has just fallen out of the top cupboard. And before we start to clean it up, we want to make sure we're wearing the right shoes so that we don't cut our feet.

A lot of us are about to turn up at the parade without the band, so the thinking has to make that dramatic shift before we consider re-attaching the nuts and bolts, otherwise it will simply fall apart.

This chapter helps give context to where we *were* and where we are *now* — allowing us all to *get it*. And only then can we move forward by *resetting, restoring and rebuilding*.

Now that we've looked at the radical changes in the ways we've been communicating, let's have a look at some of the natural ways the human brain has found to close other gaps, be creative, innovative and highly profitable.

Have you ever noticed how the first generation of immigrants in any country are often the wealthiest, in contrast to subsequent generations? There's an expression:

 Riches to rags in three generations.

Why is this?

It all comes down to an understanding of embedded processes or accepted habits, and what I like to call Immigrant Thinking.

That's all coming up next!

TWO

Immigrant Thinking

THAT'LL NEVER WORK HERE!

 Different games with different names, what happens when worlds collide and why we say "this will never work here!"

A lot of how we think is *embedded* — much of it by the age of seven. Most of what we have learned by then has been handed down to us by our parents and we tend to take on their beliefs. They received everything they know from their parents and Mom and Dad can't hand down what they don't know.

Immigrant thinking is about removing ourselves from these *embedded processes* and habits in order to survive in a new environment, similar to that of an immigrant.

If we look at immigrants who go to any country, the first generation of immigrants is usually the most successful. Why?

They went with no preconceived ideas about how things *should* be done, and *imported what worked in their old country* into their new environment.

Mostly we tend to think of immigration in terms of geography, but our immigrant thinking concept also works across different industries. Many successful entrepreneurs simply took something that worked in one industry and introduced it to another industry that was stuck in its ways.

While a *local* might think 'Oh *that* would never work *here*', immigrant thinking might be: 'Well, if *that* worked in Greece, why wouldn't it work *here* in the US? And if *that* worked in New York, why wouldn't it work *here* in LA?'

Ryanair famously imported into Ireland the low cost travel model introduced by Southwest Airlines in the US, changing forever the way the airline industry worked.

As you travel around the world, watch how people do things in different countries in inefficient ways. And the question always has to be: *why*?

Why would someone do something a certain way when it could clearly work better if done *differently*?

If Australian cafes and restaurants provided free Wifi they'd sell a lot more coffees and muffins. People would hang around longer rather than get annoyed and go next door to American-owned Starbucks for free Wifi.

If American bars removed the stools that run along the outer side of a bar, making it easier for people to order drinks, they would triple drink sales — *ask me how I know*.

Asian tourism mainly comes from Western countries where it's customary to add salt to meals as a condiment — yet it's not available on the table at most restaurants in Asia.

So immigrant thinking is more than simply taking processes from one country where they've been accepted, into a 'new' country with different habits or customs.

It's about *creating new processes*. And it's about *looking at any idea, task or problem with a set of fresh eyes*. As humans and social creatures, we tend to copy each other. We observe how something is done and then do it the same way.

While this is a nice and efficient way to go through life without having to invent the wheel over and over again, it also creates habits that are hard to break. And these embedded processes or habits can get in the way of creative thinking and innovation as well as becoming outdated.

In order to develop immigrant thinking, we don't need to come from overseas.

Immigrant thinking simply means remembering to *look at things in search for the best solution* and not just the automatic or standard one.

We should always be asking ourselves: *Is this the best way to get the job done or just the way it's always been done?*

This is a great mantra to use as we go through life.

So stop! Look at the processes you're employing now. Where did they come from? Where did you learn them?

We often accept the embedded processes of the previous generation and if we're not careful, we can also become trapped by their limitations.

It's like a snowball — it either gets better with each generation. Like in New Zealand where the mantra '*to find a way*' is handed down through generations, a belief also shared by Americans. Or the opposite, such as Australia which is infected with an anti-entrepreneurial mantra known as as 'tall poppy syndrome', a legacy from its years as a British penal colony - where anyone who is seen to do well and better themselves is 'cut down to size' by their peers.

Go to any restaurant, diner or other food place in the US, and you can modify your food order any way you could possibly imagine. And if you're prepared to pay the price, you can have it *your way*, as that's the American way.

So what is the American way?

I started buying properties from the US Government

Resolution Trust Corporation during the Savings and Loan crisis in the late 80s and early 90s. And the further west you travelled, the simpler the paperwork associated with property transfer. The Eastern states used the standard old English style, whereby the taming of the West required simple one page documents to get things done fast. The American attitude passed down has therefore been, *what needs to change to get things done, we change.*

Immigrant thinking provides a fresh prospective

Shortly after I got married in the US to a wonderful American lady, it was time for the extended family to take a once in a lifetime trip to Australia so they could do things such as ride a kangaroo and cuddle a koala.

We flew up to the Sunshine Coast and decided to visit the Big Pineapple, an area where Australia grows pineapples and where the kids can ride the pineapple train.

At the end of the day, I suggested we buy as much pineapple juice as we could carry and have a party at home. *'Take home pineapple juice'* was being advertised everywhere on signs. So imagine my astonishment when they told us we could only buy pineapple juice in small plastic cups. That was all they had. The only option to buy in bulk would be to buy and carry 27 small cups of sticky pineapple juice. Well, you can imagine that didn't appear to be the best solution.

When I suggested to management that they could sell more pineapple juice if they made it available in larger containers - especially for the many Americans that visit - the response was that not having larger ones was one of the things that made Australia unique.

Not one to get angry, only ever disappointed, I suggested that now might be a good time to introduce the Pineapple Park to the *international take home pack*.

'Take me to your kitchen,' I commanded. And there I found a large disused bulk ice cream container that I filled to the brim with pineapple juice. 'Here's your take home pack,' I said. That was about 20 years ago and I used the pictures of my international Big Pineapple Bucket for many years when teaching immigrant thinking. The good news is I believe the Pineapple Park has now introduced a more refined take home Big Pineapple Bucket.

A great case in point is the story of Tesla. Elon Musk understands the importance of being an immigrant thinker. He entered the car industry with no previous experience or embedded process about making cars. Never having learned the *standard* way, he didn't know what he was doing was considered the *wrong* way. But not only did he make the commercial electric car viable, his marketing budget is not in the billions or even multi-millions like other car companies. It's next to nothing, as you order your car online.

66 **All truth passes through three stages. First, it is ridiculed, second it is violently opposed, third it is accepted as being self evident.**

Arthur Schopenhauer - German Philosopher 1788-1860

Be different or be forgotten

THE EXTRA PEPPERONI!

- *Everything in life is simply an undiscovered process and you just need to find a way*
- *Think like a new immigrant even if you aren't one!*
- *Challenge what is 'standard' in your business or interest and ask yourself why is it 'that way'?*
- *Think about processes or 'standards' you can bring from another industry or field*
- *Look at the daily processes around you — some of them are fine tuned to be as logical and smooth as yesterday*
- *I always like to say: 'You're only as smart as your five closest friends.'*

Embedded Thoughts and Processes

TO TEA OR NOT TO TEA, THAT IS THE QUESTION

My mother loved tea. She would insist on brewing it in the teapot as she firmly believed that tea bag tea did not taste the same. For many years we sat at the table and stared at the teapot waiting for the loose leaf tea to brew. But even when it was ready, before we could pour it out, my mother would turn the pot three times clockwise to complete the process — heaven forbid anybody who poured tea from an unturned pot in her presence.

My mother always said she learned it from her mother and it made the tea taste better. One day while my mother went away to the kitchen I sneaked some tea from the still unturned pot. It tasted the same to me.

So where does this all come from?

**The inability to change can have disastrous
consequences — The Battle of the Somme 1916**

Let's look more closely at the thought process. We've just covered the concept of immigrant thinking. People bring new ideas, thoughts and patterns to a market which already has its own established thought processes. And they make changes to those processes.

Why do they have such a hard time convincing the local population, who will still say —

 'It seems like a great idea.'
'Smells like a great idea.'
'It sounds like it works over in your country.'
'... But it would never work here in ours.'

Your new tomorrow cannot be the old today

Why is that? Well, we have to understand how the brain works. The brain is made up of a number of sections, from which various thought patterns emerge.

There is no one part of the brain responsible for dealing with all thoughts, speech and logic.

But for simplicity's sake, we're going to talk about where *ideas and processes* come from.

Front Bit, Back Bit

THE SUPER SIMPLIFIED VERSION OF OUR BRAIN

When we were babies, our head resembled a big shell with absolutely nothing in it. Although we're born recognising our mother's face and smell, the first external thing we learn is the crying process.

This is usually because we're hungry or unhappy. But we soon learn that crying brings attention from Mom and Dad. And the reward is food, cuddles or a diaper change.

Then we also learn to chew food when it's placed in our mouth. But as you know, that takes a while and that's why we're given baby food to eat. Food with all the lumps smushed out, because we haven't yet learned the process of chewing the lumpy bits before swallowing — and of course we don't actually have any teeth.

The other thing we have to learn is how to walk. Now the average baby tries about 2000 to 2200 times to walk but in the meantime keeps falling down. Once she starts to walk at around 12 to 15 months, she's learned what's known as the 'walking process', even though a two year old still falls down on average 38 times a day.

So she sticks this process in the Back Bit of the brain where it stays as an *embedded process*. What's fascinating is that once a baby can walk, it will never walk any differently.

That's why you can walk down the street, see a guy you last saw when you were six years old and think 'Hey, that's my friend Barry up ahead of me.'

Because you've recognized Barry's walk and Barry cannot change it. He walks like Barry and can't walk like somebody else now because of the *embedded process* in the Back Bit of the brain.

And as he keeps walking it's like scratching into a stone tablet. Each time you scratch harder into the stone. So by the time you're an adult, this process of walking is embedded so deep into the tablet that you could never come up with another way to walk.

And if someone actually said to you, there's another way to walk, but you've got your tablet, you think to your-self: 'There isn't another way to do it. This is how it's been done. For millennia.'

As we learn these processes, they go into this Back Bit of the brain. Every time you want to do something, it's like your computer's *cache*. Rather than learning it each and every time, we've got the *cache* in the Back Bit of the brain.

'Ah, let's grab this apple from the fruit bowl, this is how I eat an apple.'

I literally grab *that* process.

'How do I put my watch on?' — I grab *that* process.

'How do I clean my teeth?' — I grab *that* process.

Now, it's so powerful in the driving structure of the brain that if you asked somebody to clean their teeth without thinking, you could actually blindfold that person and they could still clean their teeth. Because it's just an *embedded process*. No new thought needs to go into that process in order to get the *standard* result.

But what if told somebody, *'Now clean your teeth with your other hand?'*

They would probably clean their nose or eyebrows before actually placing the toothbrush into the mouth. Because it's not an *embedded process*.

As we go through life, we lock in these *embedded processes*. When we start to drive a car with a gearbox, we crash through the gears of Dad's car as we learn how to go from gear 1- 2 -3 - 4 and so on. By the time we've been driving a few years, our friends can talk to us while we drive. We can change gears effortlessly without giving it any thought whatsoever, because it's done automatically from that *embedded process*.

 If you say to a room full of people 'Cross your arms', no one has to think about how to do it. But try asking them to fold their arms the opposite way round. You'll see everybody stumble and fumble, because they have no embedded process for that way of arm folding.

When we're young we don't listen to our parents and their *embedded processes*. We have learned our own processes that work for us. They're simpler and more fit for purpose for our generation and we'll use those processes, thank you very much. We don't want to be polluted with their old outdated *embedded processes*.

So here's what's important to remember. Everyone has an *embedded process* for every repetitive action and thought. And in order to get someone to change their *embedded process* we first have to understand what it is, and then find a way to get them to change it themselves.

Because if you just *tell* people they're wrong, you'll be as popular as the host at a steak-less BBQ. No one's going to want to do business or go out with you — especially to eat.

Don't just take my word for it! Try telling your partner he's wrong and I'll meet you up on the fluffy clouds!

Because that would be trying to change someone's belief systems and *embedded processes* which are extremely rigid. We have to look and understand *processes*.

- ***How it works in business***
- ***How it works with individuals***
- ***How to introduce it so others are willing to adopt it***

Modern businesses will often unfairly value youth over age and experience because they understand that the flip side of the coin of *experience* is — *stuck in the old ways*.

If you're a business owner, call in the youngest member of your team and ask them what they would do differently. You'll be surprised.

Businesses these days are fast replacing staff who don't keep up with technology. If you're an employer you should streamline all your processes to remove those who refuse to move and think differently.

If you're an employee, you needn't be worried about that last statement because you can go to your boss and explain why process x could be so much better in your company if it became process y.

Ask this question: *'If I saved the company a whole bunch of money, how much of it would be fair to end up in my pay packet?'*

In times of economic crises like the current one, it can be hard for business to write out big cheques. So it may simply be a case of asking *'what can I have for free?'* as quite often, *time off* or an extra week of paid vacation can be of greater value to you than cash.

Where do our thoughts come from?

In the next section I'm going to give you an introduction to the Thought Box. What is it? In fact it's just the brain but the term Thought Box works better in order to understand the rest of the book. The Thought Box consists of a number of sections. And each section has different thoughts, understanding and skill sets on how to deal with all sorts of things.

 So Rick, why do I need to know this stuff?

A/ because we're about to change the way you access and use it

and

B/ if you're going to drive off into the desert you really need to know how to change a spare tire.

So pay attention...

Some sections of the Thought Box are totally empty about some subjects, while others are simply overflowing with processes and ideas.

Here's an analogy. When a person goes clothes shopping there isn't just one store, but various store with their own answer as to what the ideal suit or dress should look like.

If we understand where thoughts originate, then we can influence the subconscious mind to 'shop at our favorite clothes store'.

This way we can suggest or influence where the thoughts need to go, based on the answers we hope and expect to get back.

I'm going to share with you how we access these bits and provide you with the associated tools.

The reason you'll need these tools is because going forwards nothing will ever be the same again. How we work will be forever changed. Our personal finances will be structured differently. And we'll question our own set of values, as well as the time we now make for others in our lives.

When this COVID-19 crisis hit us, I realized that many people —like you reading this book — could be experiencing the devastating effects of having your whole world turned upside down. I decided to write this book to help you see what may not be obvious right now, and that is how to reset, restore and rebuild your life after a crisis.

Destroying my own multimillion-dollar business didn't happen overnight - it took years of practice. Fortunately I'd done it before. It's learning and understanding the following tools and ideas that will put you on the road to recovery.

THREE

The Blah Blah Blah

Starting along the road towards giving, not taking

A *script* is a piece of language or kind of conversation in which the outcome is universal and predictable. So universal in fact that we never need to think about it. It is pre-determined, automatic and already embedded in the Thought Box, just waiting to be triggered. And so much of what we do on a daily basis is controlled by scripts.

Our brains are very good at creating shortcuts to save energy on repetitive tasks. These scripts have been developed and used by us over millennia and they are not limited by language or culture. But, what if we could recognize how these scripts work and just like computer hackers inject a bit of our own 'code' into our scripts to hijack them and get the results we need?

Let's get into what triggers scripts, where they come from and how they can unknowingly influence a person's thoughts. Most importantly, let's find out how to avoid or modify them to suit our purpose.

For example, you walk into your work environment and colleagues will automatically start the 'how are you?' script. We go into McDonald's and are asked the 'would you like a drink and fries with that?' script. We return from a business trip and we get the 'what did you buy me?' script from the kids.

Barry Mumbles: 'How are you doing?'
    You: 'Great! You?'
    Barry Mumbles: 'Yeah, *great*!'

These are the standard script answers expected to the script question and you'll say all of this automatically.

There'll be no thinking — either emotional or logical — before you answer. The answers will come right out of the script bit of your brain, the Back Bit of the Thought Box.

Likewise, our friend Barry will not hear the answer, as he already has your response programmed. The response may differ culturally — more miserable folks like the British will often say 'not bad', for fear of anyone thinking things were actually 'good'.

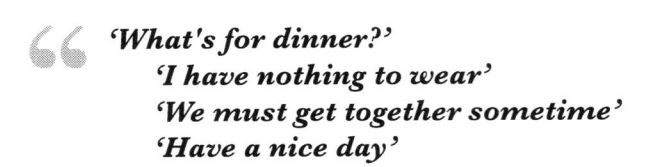

> *'What's for dinner?'*
> *'I have nothing to wear'*
> *'We must get together sometime'*
> *'Have a nice day'*

Not only do we not think about it, we don't even hear it.

Just to test and prove this concept, next time you go into work, or any environment where people know you, try this script instead.

Colleague: 'How are you doing?'
You: 'I'm dead! You?'
Colleague: 'Yeah, great!'

Even if your colleague notices your response was different, they'll be unable to stop themselves from completing the standard script. They may stop as soon as they speak and realize something was not quite right. But so much of life is made up of scripts, as they're convenient to use without employing the thinking process of the Front Bit of the Thought Box. As we've already mentioned, our Thought Boxes are not capable of multitasking.

In fact multitasking — as we've come to accept the meaning in the modern world — is a total myth. As brain researcher Daniel Kahneman has written in his bestseller *Thinking, Fast & Slow* — what actually happens when we *multitask* is that our brains are really only moving from one focus to another. They may be doing it very quickly, but never simultaneously.

Have you ever tried reading a text while driving? Regardless of whether it's legal or not in most countries, our Thought Boxes simply cannot read a text and drive a car, let alone change gear at the same time — ask me how I know this!

Scripts are very powerful and we need to learn and observe them to understand them. Otherwise our lives can become mini disaster zones.

One of the ways to persuade and influence others will be learning how to *disrupt* the standard scripts and *replace them with new ones that will produce the response that you want.*

Let me share a story with you.

Barry recently caught up with me at a function and he looked exhausted. So I asked him what was wrong and he said,

'Rick, the other day I had pizza for dinner, then jumped into bed, falling sound asleep. At about 1am, Betty snuggled against me and whispered into my ear 'I love you'. So of course I said 'I love you too'.

Then she said to me 'no, but I *really* love you...'. I thought about it for a second, realized how warm I was in bed and how cold the garage was going to be to sleep in. Then I said what any guy would say in the situation: 'Well I *really, really* love you, too'.

Then *she* said 'Really? If you *really* loved me, you'd pop downstairs and take the garbage out because I forgot it's garbage collection tomorrow morning'.

I told Barry that this is a common script, of which there are many similar ones. And I suggested that next time Betty mentions she loves him at 1am, his best answer would be a simple 'ok' or 'awesome'. Because that breaks the script and it doesn't result in 'take the garbage out'.

You may well find in the morning that your eggs are cold and the toast is burnt because you didn't take out the garbage, but this is just an example so you get the idea.

Quite often when we use a script, we say it automatically — usually triggered by somebody's words or an embedded thought. In conversations with others, you need to break the scripts or you can become a victim to the standard outcome.

Embedded scripts tell us a lot about what someone is thinking about a subject or a situation, without the person having given much conscious thought to it at all. It's just a reaction that has been triggered, but it tells us about a past or *embedded process*.

How often have you ever had someone react to something they see or hear with a script that makes you think to yourself:

 'Wow, there's a lot going on there!'

You may be out with a friend from work and casually mention you met with a banker earlier, to which he exclaims: 'Cocaine snorting thieving creeps!', and you see him tense up as he says it. So you get the idea there's a story there but it may not be the right time to ask more about it.

If you remember back in the introduction I briefly mentioned the conscious and the subconscious minds. It's the subconscious mind that gets the 'hunch' about the banker's comment, but it's the conscious that verbalizes the thought.

It's the same when Little Chris lies to Betty, who tells him:

'Now Christopher Mumbles, look me in the eye and tell me, where have you really been?'. Betty gets a hunch about whether Chris is lying or not by noticing the shrinking or dilation of his pupils. She may not have the skill set to interpret what she sees at a *conscious* level, but the *subconscious* gets a hunch and passes that to the *conscious*.

It's being in control of these thoughts and the thoughts of others in a time of crisis that calms the mind, removes the anxiety and allows for forward movement.

Ok, now where were we?

Even You, Dear Reader Are Using Scripts

 **'I don't use scripts!', you might shout
as you read this.**

But yes, you do. Always.

We use scripts like a magician uses diversions to focus your attention elsewhere so you don't see him pulling the cards out of his pocket.

We're normally powerless to react in any other way when someone uses a script on us, because we're not taught to notice or deflect them. We also use them on others without thinking or consciously planning a specific outcome or result.

Everyone around you will have been using them on you too. Your kids, your partner, your boss, the sales assistant, literally everyone around you.

And it's our response to these common scripts that usually gets us into trouble, doing things and saying things we wish we never said or did.

> *I remember being in Atlanta, GA once and as I got off a bus the driver said 'have a nice day' which is a common script in the US. However, instead of saying thank you I said 'pardon?'*
>
> *And the bus driver said 'you heard!'*
>
> *I guess I broke the 'getting off the bus in Atlanta' script!*

Be aware of the scripts

Break the script, crack the code!

So, the first thing you need to understand is *how to break those scripts so you stay in control of any situation or conversation.*

You can easily learn how to recognize scripts and then develop answers which leave the other person without a controling position in the conversation. This then allows you to take the conversation in another direction.

Customer service representatives are trained in forcing the word 'no' on us so that they can terminate the call or online chat.

When the overworked rep asks you 'is there anything else I can help you with today?', your default answer will almost always be 'no thanks'.

Because the chances are you've already had your rant about your Amazon package being thrown into your pond, or your gas bill being way too high.

This immediately gives them permission to end the call and move onto the next customer.

 Recognize what a script is and don't fall into the routine of answering the script. That's when you get manipulated by the other person and end up doing things you don't want to do.

The secret to controling the influence of scripts on your actions is to leave the speaker playing tennis against a curtain. This is done by not buying into it or returning the serve.

If someone ever says to you 'you're totally useless. You never do anything.' — this is a common script waiting for you to counter it, before receiving an onslaught of more embedded scripts.

When you answer this with a typical 'yes I do, I washed your car the other day', or anything else that directly responds and plays along with this script, you're now opening the door to even more scripted conversation:

- 'You're a useless pig who never does anything'
- 'I don't know why I married you'
- 'Mary's partner always helps her'
- 'I'm always getting stuck with the washing, ironing, cooking, looking after the kids'

Better to say 'You're absolutely right, but I am doing my best to *x.*' It's hard to argue with anyone 'doing their best'.

The Double Sure

Now that we're starting to understand embedded scripts, we can have some fun with them.

Here's a personal favorite. You go out for dinner with your partner and another couple. When the bill arrives, you pick it up, the other guy says '*look it's my turn, let me get it*' and you say '*sure?*'.

The other guy hears the word '*sure?*' and says '*yeah*', at which point your standard script response is to object. You're supposed to now say the word '*sure?*' again, followed by '*no no, let's split it*', then have a discussion about how you're going to split the bill.

This happens in all situations when two or more people have to pay a restaurant bill. I refer to it as the '*double sure*' because after the other person says *'look it's my turn I think, let me pick it up'*, he or she waits for you to reply with the second *'sure'?*. But instead, you simply say *'oh, thank you'* with a smile. You could also add *'that's very kind of you'*.

When the bill has been paid and both couples are in their cars going home, the other guy's partner will say *'why did you insist on paying the whole meal? He would have split the bill with you'* and he will respond *'I really don't know how that happened'*.

Meanwhile, in *your* car your partner will say to you *'I'm really surprised they offered to pick up the whole bill. It's so unlike them!'*

So this script, like every other script in our daily lives, has a formula. And when you break a script, you can take it in a different direction and control the outcome.

I Want to Eat Now *vs* Who's Hungry?

Let's imagine you're out with a group of friends and you're starving. Telling friends that you want to stop somewhere to eat could make you appear demanding. So let's look at a better way to get the same result by using embedded scripts.

'Who's hungry?' or *'When did everybody last eat?'* or *'What did everybody have for lunch?'* will bring up the image of food in their minds. And those who haven't had lunch will be reminded of it and feel they need to eat something. Others will say *'I wasn't, but now that you've mentioned it, who's up for stopping at the Blah Blah Blah to grab some food?'*

You can see now it wasn't *your* suggestion to eat or even make plans to stop the car to eat. Or *was* it?

Can I Give You Some Constructive Advice?

Have you ever had anyone ask you *'can I give you some constructive advice?'*

Offering constructive advice will have most people see red and pull out the *'how dare you tell me what to do'* script.

You're basically telling the other person, *'I'm right and you're wrong because I know what I'm talking about and you don't'.*

How much better it would be if you had *'some thoughts to share with you in order to get your feedback'.*

For example, *'what I've heard works well in this situation is blah blah blah'.*

Notice that in this statement it's said from the position of the *reporter* of the information. This way if the screaming starts, it didn't come from *you*, you were merely passing on what you heard from *elsewhere*. As the expression suggests, people generally don't shoot the messenger.

This allows others to pull the information rather than having it pushed at them. We've all been in situations when someone wants to influence our thinking but so as not to seem overbearing, he or she will report on what has worked for others.

How To Give Advice - As the Authority

How To Give Advice - as the Reporter

Recently I was on a vacation with my partner and I decided I would take control and book the accommodation.

My partner mentioned that when our friends go on vacation they always check the accommodation reviews before booking.

Looking back at this, that probably wasn't true. Plus it couldn't have been true because we don't have any friends.

> **A great technique to have people pull information rather than have it pushed at them is to start a story with the words "just suppose" or "just imagine". These expressions introduce ideas that others can pull and turn into their reality, rather than you convincing them of it.**

Please note, following embedded scripts is dangerous when entering uncharted waters. It's hard to avoid simply re-using other people's scripts. When they are positive ones that's fine, but we tend to resort to using other's negative scripts — most of which can be hearsay or have no real basis in reality. With most opinions presented in the negative, it does not make good fuel for the Thought Box.

Some scripts that you'll hear in today's environment:

'It's not normal procedure/policy'
'I'm sorry, but we have company rules so we won't be able to assist you'
'He/She is not interested at this time'
'Unfortunately you have a

lease/agreement/contract etc that does not allow for adjustments'
'We have no vacancy'
'We only do things x or y way'

All these are common scripts which will manipulate our thought processes if we simply accept them as delivered. At the end of the day we do not ignore them but simply accept them for what they are and move forward accordingly, as we will see later in the book.

The Three Stooges - Er, Um and Ah

When we have conversations most of the time we are giving real time thought to our responses and making them as we go along. This process naturally makes us hesitate often when we speak. *Er, um, ah* and even pauses are part of our natural speech patterns.

So, how do we know when people are using scripts as opposed to using their Thought Box to carefully compose their sentences based on real time thinking?

Generally speaking when someone responds to you and doesn't pause, or *um* and *ah*, it's because they're using an embedded script.

For example when you ask your partner 'Do you still love me?' he or she will usually respond 'yeah, of course'. The response is embedded and no conscious thought is required. The statement is almost blurted out in one complete piece.

If they do respond with an 'Er, um, well, yes, I, erm, think I do, erm, yes' then you know they are making a conscious decision about their words on the fly and you might want consider taking that conversation further.

Think about the difference between the effect of those two responses.

It's important to remember that it is not just the words we use but so much more about how we *say* them. For example, if you are going to talk to your boss about getting more money, you need to prepare your own script but what you can't do is turn up and say 'Boss, give me a raise. I've been thinking about it and prepared this speech to talk at you'. Your boss is going to feel cornered and have no input into the conversation and have a knee jerk reaction to being put on the spot.

Of course you need to know exactly what to say before you walk in, but you also need to make your boss feel involved in the discussion.

In the audio examples of scripts that come with this book you will hear me using some of the scripts I will show you later on, but you'll also notice that I'm *um-ing* and *ah-ing* like crazy. If you weren't on your way to being an expert by reading this book you'd most likely think 'what's up with Rick? I thought he was supposed to be a master at this script stuff?'

The truth is that when I use my scripts I don't need to practise anymore. I know exactly what I'm going to say for each situation, but, if I just blurted out my script like a parrot no one would ever feel like they were part of the process of getting to the answer that I want or need and would lack sincerity.

By introducing *ums* and *ahs* into my scripts it will always appear as if I'm using my Thought Box in real time, creating a thought and weighing up carefully what I'm about to say. This helps create a rapport with the person on the other side of the conversation.

If you want to see a master at work then search on YouTube for clips of Columbo. The detective character was a master at seeming to stumble over his words when really he knew each word was like an arrow hitting the bullseye. You can literally see there is only one result and the fun is watching the murderer realize that their own answers are giving Columbo a confession.

So one of the ways that we can hack the scripts we all use is to introduce hesitation in the way we deliver the phrases so that the delivery appears more natural and it gives the other person an involvement in arriving at the answer that *you* want, but that *they* are helping you reach.

Later, we will see how questions, and framing statements as questions, can help enormously to bring your scripts to life and seem just like regular, off the cuff conversation. Instead of barging into your boss' office with an agenda, you'll be more like two people standing around, each licking an ice cream, and having a chat about *stuff*. Stuff that likely ends up with you getting what you want.

I'm a Transaction Engineer

OR 'I FIX PARACHUTES THAT DIDN'T OPEN'

In the 1970s, my father headed up Qantas airlines in the US. He told me how the Americans had solved pay crises by offering everybody a job title — realizing that perceived importance often matters more to employees than money.

We all have pre-programmed thoughts and views on subjects, people and occupations. So a used car dealer or realtor could trigger a thought in another person's Thought Box that this person is lower than a snake's belly.

It explains why sales people working in advertising are called *account executives* and gas station attendants are *petroleum transportation engineers.* And why you're *unemployed* when you're at home, but *self-employed* when you're overseas.

So when people used to ask me about my work, I never used to say *'I buy and sell houses'.* I would simply say I was a *'transaction engineer moving people from yesterday to tomorrow'.*

The *framing* of that becomes really powerful. When someone hears *'I buy and sell houses'*, they have an immediate embedded scripted response, thinking they *'know'* so much about me.

But when I say I'm *'a transaction engineer moving people from yesterday to tomorrow'* , it's unusual enough to force the other person to think. And when they find they don't have any embedded thoughts on this, they'll be open to using some new thought processes to understand what I do.

So we need to use words and phrases in our communication which provide a positive outcome and paint a more appealing mental picture for others to understand.

How to Throw a Boomerang

AND MAKE SURE IT COMES BACK THE WAY YOU WANT

Let's now look at the *Law of Reciprocity*.

We all view life through our own eyes and not that of the fixed, logical bigger picture. This makes no sense but as we already know, humans are not logical.

People will always want to 'balance the books' and never feel they owe something to anyone. We all know examples of the Law of Reciprocity in action.

Your neighbour Betty offers to look after your cat while you're on vacation. Now when she tells you they're going to Greece, you feel obliged to suggest that you feed Little Chris' pet ferret in return.

And that's all reciprocity means. It simply means *in return*.

In *return* for me buying you a cup of coffee, you may feel obliged to help me figure out this income tax form that makes no sense to me.

In *return* for me putting in a good word with the boss about your brilliant ideas, you might cover for me when I need to take a day off to watch Aussie rules football (not that that will ever happen!)

In fact it's a pretty big subject and would fill a whole book. In the context of this book, the Law of Reciprocity is a complex type of script we all tend to follow. Let's look at it a little bit closer, but know that we're really only going to scratch the surface.

 People will do things for you when they feel you've done things for them.

Who does it first?
Who makes the first move?

Well, why wait? One of the best ways to prepare other people is through *pre-suasion*. That's like *persuasion* but setting things up in advance instead. There's a great book called Pre-Suasion by Robert Cialdini if you want to read more about this — check out the reading list at the back of this book.

So don't wait for others to do things for you first. Just go ahead and help people. Give advice and generally be helpful. It's like casting bread on the water. It'll come back to you when you need it.

An extreme example can be seen at the beginning of the original Godfather movie. It's Connie Corleone's wedding day and Don Corleone has to follow the tradition of granting favors and help to *anyone* who asks. So he has a long queue of people asking him for all kinds of favors. But the Don is not so bothered, because what he's really doing is setting these people up for future help when *he* needs it.

. . .

'I can do this for you Luigi, but at some point I may come to you and ask you do a favor for me in return.'

'Me do you a favor, Don Corleone? I can't see how that could ever be possible, but sure, of course I will.'

If you've seen the movie, you know the favors Don Corleone asked in return. And that's how human beings are — we're hardwired to help other people.

The Law of Reciprocity At Work

People will always feel obliged to give you something in return when they have received something from you. And where possible they'll match the value. But what's the value? This is where we can introduce some neat lopsided transactions — because we all value favors and experiences differently.

What do I mean by lopsided? Well, it's simple really. We can create win-win situations simply by understanding that the other person with whom we're communicating has different opinions, framing and most importantly their own idea of financial or monetary value.

For example, think of someone who has a different idea of '*good value*', who thinks it's fine to spend what you might consider a high price to buy something they love and value. Perhaps your version of 'good value' is the 2 for 1 offer at the upmarket cosmetics store, or a buy one get one free box seat for football. But these ideas of 'good value' are very subjective. This means that when we communicate our ideas to others, we need to let go of the concept of *value* - both in terms of *actual* price and what the other person might *think* of as the value.

It's not just the price of things on which we all have different opinions. It's been shown that it's hard for us to know whether something is good value or not, because the question in our Thought Box is always *'compared to what?'*

This is why in our online world so many products like subscription software are offered in (usually) three tiers. There's often a free or basic version, a feature packed 'pro' version and a third that is outrageously expensive and way beyond your personal needs. Next time you're presented with one of these offers, note whether any of the three columns is highlighted. I'll bet you that it is. And the companies marketing their products to you have based their entire business model on betting you'll choose the one in the middle. The top tier is always a crazy price. Why? Because if you're not familiar with the price of an item or service, the seller needs to frame in your mind what's acceptable.

If that third option costs $997 a month and the middle highlighted one is $149 a month, your Thought Box will immediately frame the $149 as being reasonable when compared to $997. But it's not a factual thing, just a *mental comparison*.

So when we communicate with others, we must overestimate the value others place on things, experiences or favors.

For example, you love the Marie Kondo Japanese method of organising belongings and you could do it all day long. If your friend asks you to help, how much of a burden would it be to you? You'd probably enjoy it. But to your friend who finds it hard to be organized, this may be worth a lot, in terms of both money and favours in return.

Maybe your friend doesn't mind picking up the kids from school on the day you have gym classes?

You can see that the value we place on things is personal and subjective. Even when it comes to the price we're willing to pay for basics like a burger.

Studies have shown that it's possible to create huge value with another person when you give them an experience that is *hard* to value. If asked, they'll often guess the true value of the favor as being far in excess of its actual cost.

When you see a free download offer on Facebook and you're asked to provide your email address in return for the link, that's just the Law of Reciprocity at work. You receive a download about how to shampoo your cat (or *how to get people to give you money*) and in return the giver receives your contact information to later sell you their brand of cat shampoo. This is known as *permission marketing*, because the brands are asking for your permission to send you their sales offers.

In some cultures when at a bar with friends, it's customary that the other person buys the round of drinks following the round that you just purchased. Arguments can break out, especially amongst men, if you attempt to buy two rounds in a row. Or is this just us Australians?!

So how can the Law of Reciprocity help get you what you need when communicating with others?

Firstly, what you provide can often be less than what you receive. Or, more specifically, what you request in return has much more inherent value *to you* than it has to the giver.

Also, as we saw above, you don't have to give people things or money. Perhaps you invest your time. Occasionally, someone will stop me during the break at one of my seminars and ask me 'one quick question', but I don't even bother charging. One day they'll do something for me which will usually have more value.

Which is better? To say *'look, I'll charge you a flat $100, and I'll give you whatever you need'* — and risk the other person's concept of your value being only worth that — or you can say *'I tell you what, let me help you out. I'll give you the best I got, don't pay me anything. We can sort that out later'*.

Some years ago, I was approached by someone in the airline industry who wanted me to do a task for him. I'd normally have charged around $1,500 at the time.

He asked my fee. I told him not to worry about it, but he insisted on returning the favor. So I hinted that at some point I'd need to fly to London. Soon after that, a business class ticket arrived in the value of $6,000.

 Another time I helped someone high up in banking circles. By suggesting there was no need to pay me, they felt compelled to lower the interest rate on their loan as a thank you. And as interest rates rose at the time, the monetary value to me was considerable.

Others may have connections or access to products and services which they may regard as soft costs (meaning it costs them less than you'd pay at retail), but be of great value to you.

Many of us, myself included, fail to realize that our years of acquired experience have high value in the marketplace and we'll readily trade it for less than its true market value — while others may see your experience as carrying immense value.

When communicating your needs to others, in all conversations in life, this is called a *trade out*. When you make a statement such as *'if I can agree to do this for you, can you do this for me?'*

The skill is to *trade out what you see as having little impact on your position in relation to what you receive in return.*

One example might be agreeing to look after your neighbour's cats when they go on vacation. When you travel and need to leave your dog for a couple of days, you'll probably feel fine about asking for that favor in return. If you love cats and live next door anyway, what's the hardship to you?

When people feel indebted to you, it makes them uncomfortable. No one likes this feeling. They'll do whatever they can to remove these social obligations and debts, so they can have peace of mind.

It could be that they have some free accommodation you can use. Or they want to cook a meal for you. But, according to scientists who study this subject, the chances are very high that the other person will return a favor that has a far greater value than the amount that you would have charged for your time.

As a fun experiment, take someone out on a regular basis for a cheap sandwich and cup of coffee. See how long you can do it for before they become really defensive about the fact they have *not returned* the favor.

Always give help and information to those around you, even if they don't ask. Some of it will come back to you in the most surprising of ways.

66 *'Do me a favor!'*

How many times do we hear this? At home, at work, down the pub with friends and of course with strangers.

With strangers it's even worse because we're conditioned to be nice to everyone. But none of us have time to do *everything* for everyone else. So it's important to know what the favor is *before* you say yes.

Most of us are happy to help out automatically and agree to doing a favor without initially asking *what* the favor is — thereby allowing the other person control of the conversation.

There's a way to handle those questions with a hidden agenda.

'Can you do me a favor, Rick?'

'Well sure buddy, *but it all depends what the favor is.*'

I've asked for permission to say *no*. I've broken the script. It's not the expected answer, but it's not a rude answer.

You won't lose friends over it.

And you've set the boundaries in a polite way.

Try offering help to someone who needs it before they ask and see what results come in. You may have to get into the habit of doing this until it becomes second nature and you even forget why you're doing it.

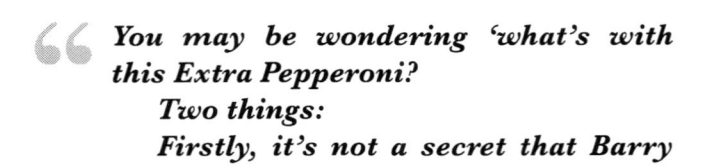

66 **You may be wondering 'what's with this Extra Pepperoni?**
   Two things:
   Firstly, it's not a secret that Barry

Mumbles is somewhat obsessed by pizza. So we thought it would be fun to add an extra something here and there at the end of a few chapters.

Secondly, we didn't want to share this fact with you until now, much later in the book, so your subconscious mind would create a thought around this and ask your conscious mind 'what's going on?'

Now you know!

THE EXTRA PEPPERONI!

Always ask what the favor is before agreeing — we'll cover this in the next section.

- *The perceived value of what you do is greater than the cost to you*
- *The Law of Reciprocity makes people feel indebted to you*
- *Intangible things can have unlimited value in the eyes of others*
- *What you give away can often pay you back tenfold*

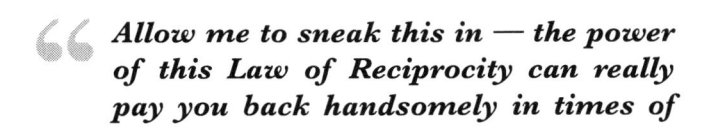 *Allow me to sneak this in — the power of this Law of Reciprocity can really pay you back handsomely in times of*

crisis - not just monetarily but can also help create vital internal tranquility for what appears to be a future of restless nights.

Always ask what the favor is first

FOUR

The Thought Box and How it Works

WHAT GOES IN MUST COME OUT, SO MAKE SURE IT
GOES IN THE RIGHT BIT!

***Why we're all so stubborn, and how to find that
'yes' and 'no' switch in every brain (without
taking it apart).***

In this section, we're going to look at which bits of our Thought Box process which types of information, and how knowing where to send our information and requests totally changes the outcome.

These days, if you have a cool new gadget and you've lost the instruction manual that came with it, there are websites that hold manuals for every device imaginable. But one thing you certainly won't find on those sites is the instruction manual to tell the Thought Box what we want it to do.

We've also talked about *embedded processes* and immigrant thinking - the stuck in the mud things that people do in different parts of the world that makes no sense other than '*That's the way we've always done it.*'

Now we're going to look a little bit at the Thought Box

and how it operates. And if you've already forgotten, we're talking about our brain!

We all tend to take our Thought Boxes for granted and never really consider how it processes information. Some of us may think it's all porridge up there and it kind of is, except with many different flavours.

You don't go to the supermarket to buy a tire for your car. It's the wrong place to go to buy a tire. Just as important - we don't ask the bit of our Thought Box for *feelings* when we need *logic*, or a set of *directions* when we're looking for *love*.

If we understand this, then it makes sense when we tap into other people's Thought Boxes, whether it be the tire or a new lover. We have to make sure we go to the right store.

When I was young Mom would drive us to the shopping mall because she needed a loaf of bread. She'd be very specific which bakery we visited and who sold fresher, tastier bread than the others. Just like the shopping mall, the Thought Box has a number of different *'stores'*. And where you choose to go to get the information you want will influence the results you get.

 Now I could have called this book 'how to speak to your brain', but that would have been as exciting as watching molasses drip down the side of a tree plus, (and you've probably already guessed by now) I wanted to tap into the correct bit of <u>your</u> Thought Box to persuade you!

Remember earlier we talked about babies learning to eat, talk, clean their teeth and so on? Well, as we grow up, we fill up our Thought Boxes with all of these *embedded processes* and it becomes harder to make room for new ones.

As a teenager fresh out of school, I was working under the wing of the Godfather of modern body language studies, Allan Pease, in a sales organization which like many others in those days invested heavily in the study of brain science. I became fascinated with the brain and how it operates. I read every possible book and article I could get my hands on to learn how people make decisions — body language, talk language, memory language, personal territories and zones, and even the association of colors and vocal tones. I instinctively knew I didn't have the instruction manual and so wanted to learn how the brain operated as part of my mission to find those missing instructions.

Scientists have now known for several decades that some people with brain injuries actually carry on about their lives relatively normally and go on about their business after recovery. Sometimes a specific ability is damaged but everything else remains the same. This is how they found out that the brain actually holds different abilities and functions through different areas.

Now, I won't bore you with all the science because it's easily available to you at the tips of your fingers with a quick Google search and down the information rabbit hole you go. There's much to learn about the brain or Thought Box, but I want to focus on just one super simplified aspect: the *Front Bit of the Thought Box and the Back Bit of the Thought Box.*

See, all of these *learned, embedded and automated processes* are stored in the Back Bit of the Thought Box. This is also known as the reptilian brain, but to make it simple let's just call it the *Back Bit*. This is the part that's slowly running out of space as we get older, because as we go through life we fill it up with more and more *embedded processes*. Some processes are necessary — others are long past their sell by date, but probably are not getting challenged in our daily lives.

Another thing you'll find in the Back Bit of the Thought Box is an automated process called the *'fight or flight response'*.

This is an internal mechanism that constantly monitors if we're feeling safe. This is really great if someone's about to punch us in the face or a flying object is about to hit our head — because that Back Bit of our Thought Box is responsible for us automatically ducking or starting to run without thinking. This Back Bit protects us in dangerous situations. It's an ancient and primitive part of our Thought Box, but it's there to help us.

How to disarm anger

What's that got to do with communicating with other people though, Rick?

I'm getting there, dear reader.

You see, that same Back Bit of the Thought Box will also protect us from questions or situations to which we don't know the immediate answer, or have enough information about. This Back Bit, which only knows how to fight or to run away, will always produce a 'no' answer to anything with which you present it.

This is really key to understanding the bulk of this book. The first reaction from the Thought Box when asked a question automatically comes from the Back Bit and the answer will be *no*! Hence the expression *'backward thinking'*.

So, when a crisis hits - whether emotional or financial - the Thought Box will by default go looking for answers from the Back Bit unless we instruct it to do otherwise. Here's where all our problems lie, and it's simply impossible to find a solution in a room full of problems.

When holding seminars I used to deliberately create rooms full of round tables. At the beginning, no one knows anyone so they would all sit wherever there was a seat. But each day I would insist they switched to a new table, so that I could observe the dynamics in the room. Sure enough, I was gobsmacked to find that the *'results'* people all sat together. And the *'reasons why we can't'* people also sat together. Each group sat together finding comfort with others who were *'just like me'*.

People would organize themselves into these groups as if telepathy was at play. Legendary author Napoleon Hill of Think and Grow Rich was convinced from his lifelong studies that we're so attracted to people who are like us that this explains things such as ghettos of poverty, or groups based on beliefs - however bizarre. This of course is also the basis of cults.

Personally, I would have sat with the *'results'* people to find out *how* they were successful - but this isn't the default state of how we operate. I share this to make you aware of it going forwards and how we solve the issues thrown up by this current crisis by becoming a *Front Bit* thinker -- building a solid foundation on which we can rebuild our lives using all the new bits of the Lego set.

The takeaway here is that to bond and build rapport with others, we tend to talk more and share stories of how bad things are with each person involved in the conversation, adding to the *wow factor*. It's likely someone will say: *'I need to find a way to turn things around or what am I going to do?'* - hoping to find a solution to the problems being discussed.

The Back Bit is incapable of finding the necessary solutions as this part of the *Thought Box* does not solve problems.

So naturally if we want people to consider anything that could lead them to giving us money or anything else, we don't want to be communicating with this Back Bit, but the Front Bit that can and will consider it.

You won't find the solution in a room full of problem thinkers

To avoid being in a room of problem thinkers, you're best to be in a room where people have paid a lot of money to be there — as the others in the room didn't make the entrance fee by being a *Back Bit* problem thinker.

As an experiment, next time you go to an educational seminar watch how the room fills up. If it's free, people will fill from the back of the room going forward. If its expensive, people will fill from the front going backward.

Moving from the Back Bit to the Front Bit

Now, it's a whole other story with the Front Bit of the Thought Box.

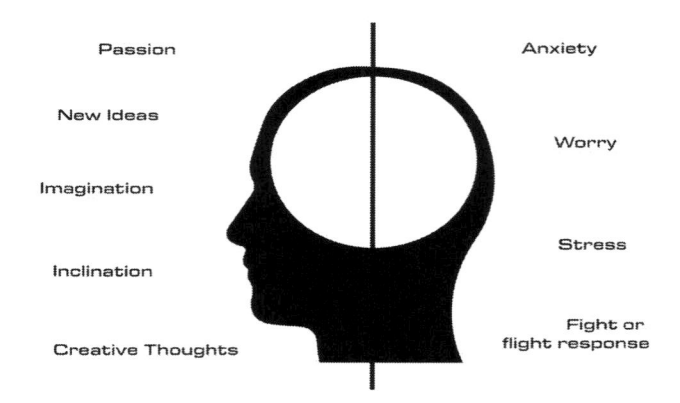

The Front Bit is where all the *good* stuff is. This is where we'll find passion, creativity, ideas, imagination and future thought. So we know that's the part of the Thought Box we want to communicate with if we want to move people towards new ideas, accept proposals, think in different ways or develop something new.

Have you ever noticed when someone has a new idea or creative thought they usually tap their forehead with excitement? That's the *Front Bit* at work!

What about when you're trying to explain something to another person and they just don't understand? Or just before you know they're going to say 'no' or something negative? They hold onto or rub the back of their head. That's the *Back Bit* that only knows how to resist new ideas and only say 'no'.

So we want to learn how to always speak directly to the Front Bit and avoid dealing with the Back Bit altogether.

And we need to ask ourselves, from which bit of the Thought Box did that thought come? Because each bit processes information differently and has different functions. So depending on where the thought came from, we'll know better how to respond to it.

Everything you know on any particular subject is in your Thought Box.

- ***'What do you think about progressive dinner parties?'***
- ***'What shall we do with Little Chris if he doesn't wash the dishes as promised?'***
- ***'How do you negotiate this company merger so we can benefit without doubling our overheads?'***

You go to your Thought Box to pull stored information. This allows you to have a conversation with the other person, and to relate your experience and knowledge about this subject.

· · ·

Now, what if I say: 'I've got this idea and here's what I'm going to do. What do you think about that?'

If you go to *your* Thought Box and it's empty, what do you think you might say in response?

You'll most likely take a negative position. The default from the Back Bit is always 'no' when you don't have a frame of reference in your Thought Box.

When you're presented with information that can't be supported by anything in the Thought Box, you may say, 'Well, I don't know.' But often in order not to appear ignorant, you'll more likely say, 'This sounds like a scam or rip off to me.'

A better answer would be 'I can't really comment on that. Because I actually have no knowledge in that area.'

This also has the benefit of making you appear more intelligent, even though you have no knowledge about the subject.

If I tell you how something works, you'll immediately look for some reference source to find evidence to support what I'm saying. Then when you have no experience or past history to draw on, you'll start to doubt that what I'm saying could possibly be real.

So, we've got to be careful about how to bring people onside with an idea when their Thought Box is empty. Hammering on about *'how things are'* to someone who has nothing in their Thought Box, to try and convince them to see our point of view, will result in an unfavorable outcome. Soon they'll be saying *'I just can't see it!'*

It's like trying to convince someone to drive a car into a pole while promising them they'll be saved by an airbag they've never seen or heard of.

First of all, people will become anxious. And then what happens? They go quiet. That's why you'll find that in business meetings or personal negotiations, when the other person starts going quiet, they're out of their comfort zone. They feel threatened and anxiety sets in. And we know that all animals become quiet when anxiety sets in. With humans it means they'll actually become less responsive to your ideas.

How does all this scripting and talk about the Thought Box help us to help others as well as ourselves? I need to take you back about 25 years ago when I was trying to buy a property in Parkland Av, Dallas. If I remember correctly it was $137,000 (weird how you remember details years later). Anyway, I wanted to make monthly payments to the seller to buy the house because as usual I had no money — or not much — and the realtor and the seller were flat out against it. The realtor was saying the seller would never agree to payments as he wanted all the cash up front and the seller was coming back with a flat '*no*'.

Not being present with the realtor when he approached the seller with my offer, I knew I had no control over the part of the seller's Thought Box from which the reply was coming. So I had to restructure the question. The conversation went something like this:

'Thanks Mr Realtor, I appreciate the seller wants all cash now and I totally understand his point of view.'
(*These comments deflate the fight or flight response in the Back Bit of the Thought Box*).
I then had to send the instruction again but this time to the Front Bit of his Thought Box where I would be less likely to get a 'no'.

'Mr Realtor, just suppose', **(*script words introducing the idea to the Front Bit for an answer*)** I were to buy his property today for the full price and he were to let me make payments — *not that he would* - (**note benefits to the seller creating endorphins and feel good energy**) — what might those payments look like? *(ask for what I want second in the sentence structure)*

'The seller has said he's not interested.'

'I totally understand, but to humor me, just suppose he were open to the idea. What might those terms be?'

The realtor returned and said, 'He still isn't interested, but if he were, it would only be for one year at 12% interest.'

'Ok, where do I sign?' I said, laughing.

There were many financial reasons why this made good sense — for discussion another time — but it was the way in which the message was communicated: with the words used, the order in which they were delivered, and the Front Bit of the Thought Box to which they were sent. The result was that the seller financed me the $137,000, so that I did not have to buy his property with cash upfront.

I Know What You're Thinking

Just imagine we had a situation where I want the Thought Box to create a thought and we can speak directly to the specific bit where this thought should come from. The result can usually be predicted.

But what if the thought was processed in another bit of the Thought Box that has different settings and options? Then the thought and response could be entirely different, right?

If we send information to someone's Thought Box and by default it gets processed by the Back Bit, we'll receive negative feedback — as well as not knowing how they felt about the information.

The Back Bit cannot house memory, imagination or creative thought. If we go to this bit of the Thought Box to get a response to a question, we will never get a humorous, imaginative or creative answer. These functions are simply not available to this bit to take off the shelf and hand back to you.

By contrast, imagination and creative thought are housed in the Front Bit, along with short and long term memory.

 Next time someone says they need some time to collect their thoughts, ask them where from!

If we understand the different bits of the Thought Box and which bits provide which types of information and opinion, then this can help us to predict a better outcome when communicating with others.

So how do we control this? How do we present an idea

or get somebody on our side where there's nothing in their Thought Box?

- ***How do we share information with someone when they have no idea what we're talking about?***
- ***How do we get them to believe in it, accept it and not be threatened by it?***
- ***How do we present this so we can get the other person to buy into what we have?***

It took me years to find the answer.

If we change the inputs correctly, then we'll get the other person to access the correct bit of their Thought Box to get their response.

For instance, if I want you to agree with an idea, I have to get you to give me your response from your ideas section in the Front Bit. Because if you go to the Back Bit of your Thought Box which houses no ideas, you'll find nothing there and come back to me and say '*no*'.

Depending on how you frame and ask a question, the other person can often just use the fight or flight response without ever actually *thinking* about the answer.

 Anxious is the man with an empty Thought Box.

So let's look at an example.

Betty: 'Do you want to go to the beach today?'

Barry: 'No.'

When confronted with new circumstances, the Back Bit goes into computing basic survival skills — your self defence and counter attack mechanisms — and the automatic flight or fight response.

The same response will also happen when presented with unsolved problems and competition from others. Neil Slade explores this in depth in his book *The Frontal Lobes Supercharge.*

The answer will be *'no'* or *'I'm too busy'* or *'We can't'*, as this bit of the Thought Box cannot re-compute new information. It can only run old, generic pre-programming, bumping into walls then turning around and playing the same old scripts over and over again.

You know the expression *'knee jerk reaction'*? When the doctor hits us just below the knee with that little rubber mallet, your leg is going to shoot forward and kick the doctor in the groin. You say *'Doctor, I'd love to stop kicking you in the groin but it's a knee jerk reaction'.*

As humans, we all like to think we're a bit special — a step up from the beasts and so on. But really what goes on in the Back Bit of the Thought Box is the thought process equivalent of that knee jerk reaction.

Depending on what and how I ask, you'll either retrieve the answer from the knee jerk Back Bit of your Thought Box with its automatic *'no'*. Or you'll be forced to consider your thoughts and then rationalise the information I've given you.

Suppose Betty wants the family to go the beach and she says 'Barry, let's go to the beach today' but Barry might respond saying 'I'm too busy today and don't have time.' Barry has simply said 'no' to Betty's beach trip question.

But, if Betty had initially asked:

'Barry, what's the best way for us to get to the beach today?'

or

'If we wanted to sneak away to the beach today, how would we do it?'

These questions would have directed Barry's Thought Box to the Front Bit for answers — or told it where to get the fresh baked bread. As a result, Barry's answers would have been more like these:

- ***'Well, I may not have time, but we could try to escape in the afternoon.'***
- ***'Well, I want to finish watching the game, and then we can see how we're doing.'***
- ***'If I had to make it work, I suppose I could record the game and watch it later.'***

Betty could have asked a different question:

'Barry, I understand you probably can't get to the beach today. So let me ask you something. Just suppose we had to find the time? How do you think we might do it? Not that we're going to, but if we had to? How do you think you'd do it?'

Now Barry's answer might be:

'Ah, well, if I had to do it, I think I'd leave straight away and listen to the game on the radio.'

If we know we're guaranteed to get a '*no*' to these questions, we can also see how if we asked another question or reframed the question, we'd have more chance of receiving a different reaction from the Front Bit of the Thought Box. A reaction that's in line with what we're asking the other person to do or consider.

Now stop! Before we go on, it's important to see if

we're all singing from the same song sheet. To summarize, good stuff comes out of the *Front Bit* of the Thought Box - whether it's ours or someone else's - and the *not so good* stuff comes from the *Back Bit,* to which we all default.

In this section we're learning specific language we can copy and use to redirect the thinking process in order to get more desirable results. For instance, happy people think happy thoughts which all originate from the Front Bit and others will want to be a part of that.

To this day, I still remember meeting my partner at a party. She was not the most attractive girl in the room but she was giving off such an incredible happy energy that she was attracting everybody around her - and I didn't want to be left out. For years people would say 'your wife is so much fun to be around'. And I understand that because of the positive energy she gives - not because she tells good jokes.

Where we go now is simple. In order to deal with the fallout from any kind of crisis, we need to reframe our thoughts and use these tools to reset, restore and rebuild towards recovery and success.

In order to avoid triggering the fight or flight response, we can use framing to fine tune our questions so that they are processed by the Front Bit of the other person's Thought Box.

When I used to speak on stage, I found that after a while I had no leverage — being limited to 24 hours in a day like everybody else. When people asked me to speak at conventions to share with delegates *how to get people to give you what you want without asking*, the question needed to be reframed so that the reply came from the Front Bit — benefitting both parties and keeping everybody feeling good while also achieving the required outcome.

'Rick, could you attend a convention and address our people on how to get others to communicate more easily and effectively?'

'Are you asking *me* to attend or asking me if I can send someone to your convention to address your people on how *to communicate more easily and effectively?'*

'Yes, the *latter!'*

A scripted embedded *'no'* response from the Back Bit of the Thought Box would have proved disastrous for the company's growth.

Reframing allows you to effectively introduce more profitable ideas, systems, processes and techniques.

**A reframed positioning statement disrupts embedded
thinking and introduces more profitable ideas**

The fight or flight response comes from the Back Bit of the Thought Box, while all the creative and exciting responses come from the Front Bit. Given a choice, we can direct people as well as ourselves to seek information and thought patterns from the Front Bit instead of the Back Bit.

Imagine you have a garden where all the weeds are at the back and the roses are at the front. Now it's Valentine's Day and your partner is about to walk in the front door. Which end of the garden are you going to pick from?

People must like you before they will do business with you

THE EXTRA PEPPERONI!

- ***Humans default to the Back Bit for responses***
- ***The Back Bit is knee jerk 'no'***

- *'How', 'Why', 'Just suppose' and 'Imagine' questions move people to the Front Bit*
- *The Front Bit houses logic, empathy, passion and all things 'forward thinking'.*

FIVE

Getting Ahead of the Game

OLD WAYS WON'T OPEN NEW DOORS

 Why Bernie Madoff got so many people and how to make people emotional and feel the love

So we've now examined the Thought Box and discussed the Back Bit that always wants to fight, run and just say 'no'.

But what about the decisions we constantly make? Whether to drink coffee, go to bed early or cross the road further along? All these things come from our emotional bit of the Thought Box.

The Emotional Bit of the Thought Box

How many times have you heard someone say *'I don't know why he does that, it makes no sense?'*

Because the person asking the question is using their

own logic to try to understand the other person's emotional thinking.

If it were that easy, we'd all know the answers to why people drive around for ages looking for the nearest parking spot to the gym entrance, why World War II kamikaze pilots wore helmets or why someone would order the Big Mac with double fries and onion rings, then choose Diet Coke.

Whenever you want someone to make a decision, you need to make sure that you're communicating with their emotional bit of the Thought Box. We actually make decisions based on emotions and only *later* do we find the logic to justify them.

If we were really logical and our decisions were not based on emotions like love, greed, jealousy or hate, then there'd be no point in the character of *Mr Spock* in Star Trek. We laugh at his inability to understand *Captain Kirk's* decisions.

Why? We can easily understand and relate to Kirk's decisions because they're human ones, based on emotion.

Spock, however, can only make rational logical decisions and cannot understand why Kirk doesn't.

This Spock example should start to get you thinking how *in reality we only make decisions based on emotions. Then we use logic to try and justify our positions*.

So how do we get people to make 'logical' decisions? We need to move them to an emotional state. Get them to take the steps to think through the arguments in their own minds. And then use the logic we present to organize and justify those thoughts.

Experiments conducted in the 1970s showed that when faced with choices in a gambling environment, most people did not choose the bet with the highest odds of winning. Even when shown the math first, they'd still choose to place bets that made no logical sense.

Take national and state lotteries. We'll buy a ticket when the prize is the largest. This makes no logical sense. Why? Because although the prize gets *bigger* with more tickets sold — the more tickets that are sold, the *lower* your chances are of winning the jackpot.

So why do we buy lottery tickets then? Because the emotional rush of imagining a joyous future from winning all that lovely prize money makes us justify the purchase of a lottery ticket using supposed logic. In this case, the logic is *'Well, somebody has to win, right?'*

We even see massive hedge funds and the so-called smartest on Wall Street fall into the trap of human decision making. It's never based on logic.

Bernie Madoff knew that when he convinced hundreds of the super rich to join his unique 'club'. Those investors also used emotional thinking and then afterwards created their own 'logic' to back up their decisions.

'Well I don't know much about what Bernie does, but if the Bernsteins are with him, then we'd be fools not to invest.'

What people are buying into is the concept of *'maybe one day in the future'*. And it's an *emotional* decision that cannot be a *logical* decision. Because nobody using only logic would invest money in a business that doesn't make money. And nobody has ever been able to predict the future outside of some lucky guesses.

So we know that decisions to act come from the

emotional bit of the Thought Box. Therefore it's important that our language changes in order to talk to it.

If you want something to make sense don't ask a human

66 *People will fear making a mistake much more than moving towards a benefit.*

So even if the odds are stacked in the favor of making a profit, we'll protect ourselves from making a mistake.

So what if people won't follow the rules of emotional logic? Well, they will. Everybody will. But first we have to get them there. And for some personality types, that's easier and for others it can be tougher.

How Would That Make You Feel?

Keeping people in the emotional bit of the Thought Box when we need them to make decisions is so important that

I'll often end a sentence with 'How does that make you feel?'

 Feelings are emotional and the value of something is based on how the result makes someone feel — not what it actually is.

When I chat to people I always include the question somewhere in the conversation — *'what would make you happy?'* — then shut up while the the other person fills in the blanks.

When they've finished talking, I finish with:

'And if we're able to make all this happen for you today, how would that make you feel?'

Once they answer I simply give them the list of what I need them to do *now* in order for me to provide them with the result they need.

If we ever meet in person or you see me speaking on YouTube, you'll notice that my language is peppered with phrases such as:

- ***'Just suppose'***
- ***'Imagine'***
- ***'In a perfect world'***
- ***'What would you like to see happen?'***
- ***'How would that make you feel?'***

If humans used logic, why would kamikaze pilots wear helmets?

One Question, Better Outcome

You can ask the same question a couple of different ways and get the same reply but a *better* outcome.

When we constantly ask people how they *feel* about the decisions we want them to make, it keeps them using the emotional bit, the decision making bit of the Thought Box. Think of stoking a campfire — you need to give the fire oxygen by keeping the embers burning. Making others *feel* is the same thing, so stoke those emotions when you're talking to them.

I never used to *sell*, I'd simply *chat* with people about solving their particular problem. I discovered that it was never about the actual widget but always some emotional element - a new job, divorce, marriage etc.

Once my assistant asked: 'Rick, how come you don't remember this buyer's name and the reason they're buying? He only told you yesterday.'

The thing is, I made a point of never keeping people's details so they would need to remind me who they were and, more importantly, *why* they were coming to see me. After the intentional confusion and much apologizing, I'd bring them back to the thinking about their *needs* and *wants*. I wanted the buyer to retell the story of why they needed to buy. So I was stoking those embers, stirring up the feelings once more. I could then address those feelings with solutions they could also *feel* made sense.

This could only be done if they saw the widget as part of their future by tuning into the emotional bit of their Thought Boxes.

I wanted them to imagine themselves in that improved space and experience, and ask how would that make them *feel*?

THE EXTRA PEPPERONI

- People make decisions more readily when they *feel* it's easy, fun and '*I can do it*'
- 'How does that make you *feel*?' — switches people to an emotional state
- Or put it this way:

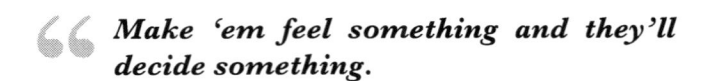 **Make 'em feel something and they'll decide something.**

Pineapple Words

We now know how words work to encourage the Front Bit of the Thought Box to consider all the options and make decisions, instead of leaving the Back Bit to say 'no'.

Let's look at how we can still get tripped up with some of the simplest, seemingly most inoffensive words out there. Pineapple Words.

Named after the World War II American pineapple-shaped hand grenades, these words have potential to blow up our negotiations in all aspects of life.

The reason this description is so spot on is because the words we use can have devastating results as they conjure up thoughts in others' Thought Boxes. Therefore our words need to be carefully chosen, so that the correct thought association is made.

Barry Mumbles will have certain thoughts about the words he hears. So to control those thoughts — even before Barry has them — we need to control the words Barry hears and have them enter through the Front Bit of his Thought Box while avoiding the Back Bit.

Let's consider the topic of *contracts*. Now there's a Pineapple Word if ever we heard one.

Contracts are often deemed as being complicated and scary. The kind of thing for which you need a lawyer. We're often taught at a very young age not to *sign* (another Pineapple Word!) anything.

If I say *'Barry, how about we get the contract signed?'*

Barry's not going to be enthusiastic because I know how people feel about contracts and signing anything. His primary emotion is going to be anxiety. *'I don't know what I'm doing. I'm out of my comfort zone, getting into something I don't know. What if I don't understand the small print?'*

There are already negative thought patterns in Barry's Back Bit of the Thought Box because I introduced two Pineapple Words:

Contract and **Sign.**

So what if rather than saying *'Let's go and sign a contract?'* I said *'Let's go get some papers organized?'*

Now, what do you think goes through Barry's mind?

'Oh it's just papers'. Something less threatening that has writing on it. *'I read it, I roll tobacco with it, I wipe my butt with it…'*

He comes across this kind of word association with the word *papers* daily. It's not a scary word.

This word *papers* instead of *contract* removes the unknown — the anxiety.

Anyway, back to this contract. By the way, could the words on the paper be exactly the same words on the '*contract*'? Yes, but again by using the wrong words, we are using Pineapple Words.

.   .   .

As I just said, Pineapple Words are words that are *loaded*. It's as if you're going to start throwing grenades at someone's head.

So when I say *'sign something'*, I'm introducing a reference to an embedded thought from the Back Bit of the Thought Box which says *'Never sign anything!!'*

Instead we can say things like, *'Let's note down what we agreed and then write our names.'* or *'Just make your mark here. A thumb print dipped in tar will suffice.'*

This is likely to elicit a little laugh and release all the built up anxiety. Another way is to sign first, then silently turn the paper around towards Barry, who will follow my example.

Now, it's not like Barry is doing anything against his will. However, by avoiding the Pineapple Words *'contract'* and *'sign'* and replacing them with words that won't trigger his fight or flight response in the Back Bit of the Thought Box, he doesn't become anxious.

I may even hand Barry the papers and say:

'Hey Barry, how do you spell your last name? Great, put that here so I don't forget in future.'

Barry will then sign in the signature box without me using Pineapple Words that might bring up thoughts with *negative* associations. This way the pin never needs to be pulled from the grenade.

Describing the benefit that a form or contract provides is more powerful than the title of a form and avoids using Pineapple Words.

Some great examples of Pineapple Words are ones associated with time. How often have you had someone tell you they'll meet you in 5 minutes and you find yourself still waiting 30 minutes later?

'I'm only 5 minutes away'
'Just a second'
'She'll be with you in a minute'

We all know that these don't reflect real timeframes. If you want to control people using a time period, making them far more likely to take notice of your meeting and turn up on time, then use odd times like:

'I'll meet you at 3.13'
'I'll be there in 4 minutes'
'Let's meet for 7 minutes'

Odd times don't trigger the embedded negative scripts associated with '5 minutes meaning 20'. They suggest to others you're a disciplined and reliable person without having to *tell* people this.

If I were going for a job interview and was asked by the receptionist what a good time would be, I would answer 3.27pm rather than 3.30pm. He's more likely to notice me and probably mention this to his boss. She'll make an assumption that I'm someone he can probably rely on.

'5 minutes' is a Pineapple Word — 7 or 13 minutes is not

'...she has a nice personality'

Think about the association people may have to certain words and whether it's positive and non-threatening. If the association is negative or likely to introduce many negative embedded scripts from the Back Bit of the Thought Box, then simply change the words.

For example, I'll never call to say I'm *running late* for a meeting. Instead *'I'm just a bit behind schedule'*. Behind schedule indicates you are organized because you work to a schedule, while *'late'* implies you're simply unreliable and disorganized.

Pineapple Words can appear on paper as well as in daily speech. Over the years many clients have asked me to review papers, letters, proposals or statements before sending them. My question is always the same: How do you want the person to feel when reading this, and what action do you want them to take? When we look at the desired outcome first, then we can remove all the Pineapple Words that get in the way.

The Thought Box has a list of scripts as to why it should *not do something* as opposed to just doing it. If you speak to the Back Bit and knock these scripts out, the Front Bit has no alternative but to move forward, as all the reasons not to have been removed.

What thoughts do your words conjure up?

Pineapple Words are super important in both personal interaction and business. They can be replaced instead with Shoehorn Words in order for a proposal to be more easily accepted in many situations.

Shoehorn Words

The harmless cousin of the Pineapple Word, *Shoehorn Words* are nice and polite. They reduce the barriers and provide the oil that helps move things through, like a lubricant for words. For instance, no one likes to *stop* doing anything and no one wants to *start* doing anything new, but we're all happy to *transfer across* or *move towards*.

Shoehorn Words allow the easy slipping in of a subject, while providing the least resistance to the proposal being made.

When somebody has something in an embedded process or script they're reluctant to stop it, because it's already in play. So if we ask them to stop doing something, they're going to ask why. It's a big decision for them to make.

If we ask a client to *stop* working with company A and instead *start* working with company B, this is a big decision to make. They've never had to do that before. We're chucking around the Pineapple Words — *stop* and *start*.

. . .

124

We know that when we throw Pineapple Words up in the air, some people will go into a fight or flight response in the Back Bit of the Thought Box.

So if we use a different phrase *'Hey, why don't we just simply transfer from A to B?'*. People will happily *transfer* across and the practicality of it being *'from A to B'* that *stops* one thing and *starts* another is entirely lost on them.

Right now, many struggling businesses need to reallocate staff. A less destructive way to do that with Shoehorn Words is not to tell people their jobs have *gone*.

It's far better to suggest that the more skills they can acquire, the more valuable they are to the company. 'And with that in mind we'd like to move you *up* to the_____ *fill in the blank* department. The Shoehorn Word here is moving people *up*, or we can use other phrases such as *upgrade to* or *progress to*.

In the worst case, if it really isn't defensible as any kind of *up*, then *sideways* is better than *gone*. To move someone sideways, you can *transfer* them *across* to department *x*.

This can be used in reverse if you're an *employee* and feel that there will be potential job cuts in your department but more security elsewhere in the organization.

Approach your boss and suggest that to *help the company in this time of need* you're happy to *step up* or *upgrade* to the blah blah blah department for the same salary *in order to do your part*. The reason this is effective is because when we *step down* we associate that with paying less, while *stepping up* has the opposite effect.

For many years I employed people and learned that the closest thing to manufactured perfection on this planet is a job applicant's resume. As an employer I'm trying to assess whether employing you will *make* me money or *cost* me money. Having to assess an individual during numerous interviews and meetings costs both time and money.

A Shoehorn conversation means you slip yourself into the job in two ways, so pay attention when you're job hunting.

1. Research and find out everything about the business you want to work for inside out. This will blow the employer away as very few potential candidates ever bother to do this. And it says a lot about your attitude without the need to be asked and tells the interviewer *why* they need you.

2. Interviewers generally follow the same familiar patterns. The normal script that pops into the interviewer's Thought Box when you say something will be: *'really, and why is that?'*. So instead, tell the interviewer how employing you will make her company more money. And use this opportunity to showcase your skills and experience by discussing how you might be able to help her.

Great Shoehorn Words to sprinkle in here could be:

'Save you money'
'Streamline'
'More profitable'
'More efficient'

What visual image are your words creating?

You may notice that I avoid using Pineapple Words in this book where possible. This is because I want to affect how you *feel* about many elements, and want you to conjure up positive, not negative thoughts.

Renaming the Pineapple Word

One way to defuse a Pineapple Word is to replace it by describing its function. This method has served me well over many years of asking others to sign forms and contracts, which as we have seen, are loaded with Pineapple Words.

These words below don't need to mean anything to you but they are typical *jargon* words, words many of us to show we're *in the know, in the club*. We expect to be recognized only by others in the same business, field or hobby — and from those who don't understand them that we want respect. But instead of using jargon to intimidate and confuse, let's describe the *benefit* a form provides. This is far more powerful and doesn't introduce those pesky Pineapple Words.

Look at these examples below. I don't expect you know the 'official' terms but I'm willing to bet you will understand them if I frame them like this.

Instead of legal jargon, I've used the terms in *italics*:

- **An insurance certificate** - *the paper that provides peace of mind 24/7*
- **Warranty Deed** - *the paper that moves you into that Caribbean hideaway*
- **Tax certificate** — *the paper that keeps the IRS happy and off your back*
- **Divorce decree** — *this little puppy allows you to be in the arms of that hunk of a man you've had your eye on at the gym*

Showing the results and benefits that forms provide to the other person brings the emotional power to the table, rather than the boring or fearful logic behind the form. When we describe it to the other person like this, we move them to the emotional bit of the Thought Box, which makes decisions.

People buy into what it *does*, not what it *is*.

Over decades of buying and selling houses, I've learned that most property sellers and buyers are really just Moms and Dads. They aren't real estate experts. They are the Mumbles.

They want to move into their future home: a new room for the baby, close to a good school, so they can have fun having more little Mumbles.

So I know that *mortgage* and *finance term* and *interest rate* are Pineapple Words. I'm taking these Moms and Dads into areas where they have no common understanding, so their preconceived ideas and thoughts are generally going to be negative, coming from the Back Bit of their Thought Boxes.

I'd therefore use words like *'the debt bit'* and *'the cash bit'*, refer to the mortgage broker or financier as the *'money guy'*, the accountant the *'numbers guy'* and equity as simply *'that cash bit you get to walk away with and put into your next home'*.

When it was time to sign, I'd stand across the table, say to Dad *'Catch this!'* and throw the pen to him. By catching it, he'd know it was time for him to sign but without me having to use any Pineapple Words.

On the other hand, if we try to ask people to fill out *'mortgage form S152'* — a form they may never have heard of — they'll try and go to their Thought Boxes to find out everything they know about *mortgage form S152*.

When they find no information or past experience of this form, they'll feel fear and anxiety. And where there's fear and anxiety, what do we have?

That's right. Deer caught in the headlights. They do nothing.

In this position, people can't go forward and can't make decisions. And to alleviate the fear they need to call in outside resources from the so-called 'experts' to help them make decisions.

Financial planners, accountants, lawyers and other people that they believe have experience with these types of forms just to help make the fear and anxiety go away. And then what happens to our deal that was going to be sealed today in about five seconds time?

It doesn't happen.

But when you say *'This is the form that says you'll never pay those debts for the rest of your life. How would that make you feel?'*

What do you think happens to Barry now?

Pen to paper and Barry signs his name.

· · ·

This way, there's almost no situation in which we can't turn Pineapple Words away from fear and anxiety and into simple benefits that anyone can understand. Because if they're simple and people can understand them, they can move forward and take action.

The term *'guests coming over'* can be viewed as Pineapple Words, as most people believe their home is a mess even if it was tidied and cleaned just yesterday.

To avoid this we can use words like *'dropping by'* as it doesn't set off the same negative embedded thoughts from the Back Bit of the Thought Box.

A lesson learned

When I was 18 I learned to drive and it wasn't long before I had my first car accident in the rain as I slid into the car in front. When I was in court — although I had slid into the car in front due to the road having been wet — when the judge asked me to explain what happened, I mentioned that I had *aquaplaned* into the car in front.

The judge said that for a car to *aquaplane* as opposed to *slide* meant there had to have been a body of water between the road and my tyres, and to have been driving in those road conditions was therefore irresponsible.

Because of that one Pineapple Word, I was charged with negligent driving and received a $50 fine. But it made me realize the importance of the words I used. *Aquaplane* had definitely been a Pineapple Word of major proportions.

The point is, you can lose money using Pineapple Words, but you can get people give you a lot more when you don't use them.

I think if it ever happened again, I'd say *'Your honor, my car simply walked up to the car in front and said 'hello'*.

My PHP Won't Talk to My ASP Because of the 123 On the Doh Ray Me

KISS - KEEP IT SIMPLE STUPID

 Jargon. Don't you just love it?

When we talk about language, we need to use words that everybody understands. I like to talk about the *12 year old Thought Box*. Which means that while some people may indeed be smarter and cleverer than others, *everybody* I speak to will at the very least have the understanding of a 12 year old.

So I speak and write using simple words, making it easy for people to respond in the way I want. And I want my words processed quickly so people don't tune out when I'm speaking. If I use language that's complicated, people will take longer to process that language, understand the meaning of my words and then respond.

What do I mean by *jargon*? I started talking about it in the previous section. It's a group of words only recognisable to a small tribe of users and unfamiliar to outsiders. Others hear these words but don't instantly recognize them or understand their meaning.

A classic example is when you take your laptop to the repair shop and the Spotty Youth with Glasses says 'Well, it's pretty obvious. I don't know why you didn't say something when you brought it in. But it's clear that your PHP won't talk to your ASP because of the 123 on the server side and https hasn't migrated yet to the DNS on the ISP.'

And you think, *'Just fix the damn thing.'*

The laptop-fixing Spotty Youth with Glasses has to show his superiority in this situation by using jargon that average people, certainly 12 year olds, would never use.

Apple understands this so much better than Microsoft. In Apple Stores, you book an appointment at the Genius Bar, take your iPad, iPhone or MacBook in and they tell you *'Don't worry. Leave it with us, grab a coffee and come back in an hour'*.

You go back and it's fixed.

Apple understands that you *don't need to know or care* what was wrong, only that it's *fixed*.

On the other hand, the Microsoft business model is all about getting independent people like our Spotty Youth with Glasses to pay for courses to learn all the jargon so they can tell their customers *just how smart they are* and keep you paying for services that sound and *feel* complex.

I once needed window shutters for my house. The salesman told me I could get wooden shutters to keep the sun out. I was about to write the cheque when his assistant decided to tell me about all the different kinds of wood available, the various types of cleaning processes and all the possible combinations. He might as well have been speaking Greek. It was all wooden shutter jargon and I didn't have a clue.

I said I needed to think about it and get back to them. Eighteen months later, I still don't have shutters.

We use jargon believing we're helping people make informed decisions. But unless people ask for specifics, it means they don't want to know. They want the *benefit* of what you know, not *what* you know.

When we use jargon with average people outside our profession, what we're really saying is — *'Don't worry, you wouldn't understand but I have massive value.'*

That's the thinking — so I'm going to use all this jargon and talk about my *ABC, 123* and the *doh ray me* and the 27 letters after my name on the business card or on my office door.

 **It's too hard, baby!**

Jargon slows the process time to 'yes'

While the Thought Box is struggling to process the jargon, the other person is still talking.

Why is all this important, especially in business?

The Thought Box now says to the mouth: '*We've not had time to process all of this yet!*'. With all the jargon it constantly needs to process, it's starting to get tired trying to process it all.

Barry would say in a meeting:

'We've had a great day today. Let's stop now because I'm getting a bit tired. Pizza, anyone?'

So if you're trying to sell Barry on your latest idea while he's trying to process all your complicated words, he'll start believing it really is all quite complicated.

Remember, in a perfect world people only prefer change towards, or *transfer* towards, things they actually believe to be easy. If we want Barry to change things, he'll only move towards that change if he feels it fits within his skill set.

For many years, car ads attempted to attract customers by describing the '*overhead valves with 340 horsepower with lots of torque down low overhead greased nipples and wrap around door handles.*' Jargon that the car industry invented but didn't realize that no one else understood.

Mazda finally figured it out what people really wanted to know about cars. They just go '*zoom! zoom! zoom!*'

People just want to *get it*. Next time you hear a friend go into detail explaining something, watch how others will cut them off and say something like:

'Come on, Barry, get to the point.'

Which really means '*how does this affect me?*' or '*I get it*' or '*let's move on!*'

If we make it easier for people to understand, it becomes easier for them to relate and they're then more likely to make the decision.

A lot of the time people use jargon to show self-importance, their worth and sharing their knowledge, so that people perceive the value in it. And they're absolutely right.

 We're aware of the salient facts underlying the altruistic nature of diagrammatic dilemma.

What?!

As we've seen, using jargon will create anxiety in the Thought Box of the average person and create an inability to move forward.

Dumbing it Down for Dummies

EVEN LAWYERS CAN UNDERSTAND SIMPLE WORDS

 Remember you're only 12.

None of us are willing to invest in something if we don't understand it. Because we all have peers, friends, business associates, partners. And we have to try to explain to someone *why we did what we did*.

If you want people to make quick decisions, the language has to be simple, fast and easy. Never complicated.

The most obvious example of people who make a living by making the simple seem complex are lawyers, also affectionately known as *deal killers*.

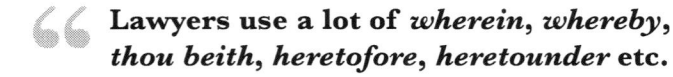 **Lawyers use a lot of *wherein, whereby, thou beith, heretofore, heretounder* etc.**

Even a lawyer can understand simple words. So let's keep everyone happy and always leave out the jargon.

Although every occupation uses jargon, only you understand the embedded parts of that language that no one else uses. Remember Barry and Betty have no points of reference in their Thought Boxes for your jargon. So they're going to have to find other people to help them understand what you've just said. 12 year old language removes anxiety which creates indecision in people.

———

Many years ago, I was buying a property and I wanted the seller to also pay my purchase taxes — which was legal, though a little unusual.

The realtor putting this transaction together had never heard of this before:

'I'm going to have to get something in writing, Mr Otton, as *all this is very unusual.*'

'Sure, no worries. Can I fax it across?'

'Yes, of course.'

I got a sheet of paper and a child's crayon and being left-handed, I wrote with my right hand.

'SELLER WILL PAY RICK'S TAXES WHEN RICK BUYS HOUSE'

Ten minutes later the realtor called back.
'Great, thanks for that. That should be OK.'

———

When you write like a child, it's hard for adults to not understand you, as the suggestion would be that a child is smarter than the realtor.

To summarise, writing and speaking in simple language that even a 12 year old can understand means *everyone* will feel more comfortable more quickly and feel far less anxiety.

THE EXTRA PEPPERONI!

- *Avoid jargon as it creates anxiety in others — find the benefits as discussed in the previous chapter*
- *Anxious people do not make decisions — the Back Bit of the Thought Box fights back*
- *Impress by making complicated things simple, not the other way round*
- *If Barry doesn't feel he can explain it to Betty, then Barry won't buy it*

The Second Smartest Man

We can see the benefits of keeping things simple when we look at the best way to position ourselves in a conversation. I like to call this the *Second Smartest Man* after the TV detective Lieutenant Columbo. Columbo solved all the murders on his show by positioning himself as the least smart person in the room.

If I make you feel like I'm the second most important person in the room, and that you're smarter, this gives me an advantage over you in any discussion. There is a *law* in life that the person who feels she's more intelligent will want to educate those in the room who are less smart to help them reach their own level of understanding. *People always want to help other people.*

So if I say 'hey Betty help me understand something here', then Betty will lean in, ready to give me the full benefit of her knowledge. It's just how we are.

So we'll talk a lot and share the experience because we want everybody to be just like us. It's the *'just like me'* syndrome. We all want everybody else to be *just like us*.

If on the other hand, you enter the room, positioning

yourself as the smartest person there, others will become defensive and be less inclined to share. If you arrive with a shiny business card, you're asking others to compete with you. And the competitive nature of humans is to attempt to outdo any other man or woman in the room for dominance.

It's a common thing on business cards or in LinkedIn profiles that people put a bunch of letters after their name to show how important they are. Even if you have those qualifications, it can be way more useful to at least appear less smart and less threatening.

Columbo always found his killer by making the suspect feel they were superior in every way, which meant they let their guard down. By asking very specific questions as the 'Second Smartest Man', Columbo was able to trap the killers by their own words. Later in the book I'll show you exactly what those questions are and how you can use them in everyday practical situations. You may not need to trap a murderer, but you can use them on your partner, kids, boss or landlord, often to devastating effect.

By being the second smartest man , there is no threat
so everybody shares and educates. I call it being
'Columbo'

Using Sentences with Benefits First

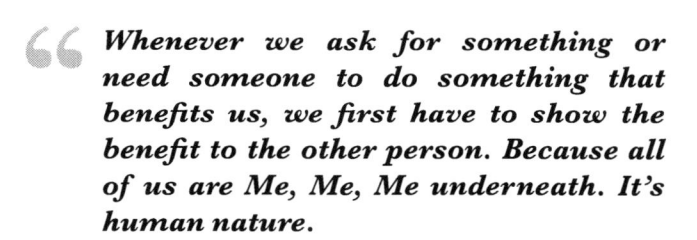 ***Whenever we ask for something or need someone to do something that benefits us, we first have to show the benefit to the other person. Because all of us are Me, Me, Me underneath. It's human nature.***

Barry's Bike

Now we all know that Barry is our mate, but let's assume he's a stranger for now.

'Barry, I know you've been trying to sell this bike for a while. But if I could get you the price you want and give it to you today (*speaking to the emotional side of the Thought Box, creating excitement*), do you think you might be able to deliver it to me?'

Barry: 'Sure, I don't think that would be a problem.'

Had I simply asked, 'Barry, will you deliver the bike if I buy it?', he more than likely would have replied 'Er no, that wasn't what I was planning. You'll need to pick it up yourself.'

But Barry heard that the deal was being done *today* and got excited by this *and* getting the price he wanted. So the benefit to me was merely a small concession.

But it would save *me* both time and gas money. Another form of hidden discount, another way we can give people what they want and still get them to 'give us money'.

If you regularly buy and sell stuff, the amount of money and time you could save by using this tactic is considerable.

The Contractor at Work

If I get a contractor to do work and ask him if I can make installment payments on the contract, he'll most certainly say *no*, he needs full payment upfront.

If I restructured the question however, I might get a very different answer — *'I'm happy to accept your price and contract and even fit in your time frame, if you can give me some flexibility with the payment structure.'*

He might respond with, *'It's not our normal way of doing business, but I think we could accommodate you if you could give us a small deposit of 10% to cover some 'getting started' materials.'*

My Beloved

Barry: 'Betty, darling! How about I help do the grocery shopping and I can have it all done so you don't have to think about it? And on the way back I'll catch up with Tom and Jerry, killing two birds with one stone."

Betty: 'Sounds good, what time do you think you'll be home?'

Barry: 'Not late.'

Barry first showed Betty the benefit to her. Watch what happens when he uses the old way of saying things:

Barry: 'Hey love, I'm going over to see Tom and Jerry.'

Betty: 'What for? What about *me*?'

Barry: 'Do you want me to pick up something on the way home from the grocery store?'

Betty: 'No, I want you to spend some quality time with *me*. You can see your friends any time.'

What's in it for the other person - the *benefit* - *must* be delivered first. The Law of Reciprocity - she's done something for me, so I have to do something for her - also comes into play here. When you structure a sentence that has you taking what you want in the second half of the sentence, the other person hears the embedded script *'you scratch my back, I'll scratch yours.'*

When you get this wrong, you'll likely trigger the person's embedded script *'What's in this for me?'*

In my teaching seminars, I'd often run over into the lunch hour.

If I said *'Guys, today's one hour lunch is only going to be 30 minutes'*, people would get annoyed because *I* ran overtime.

So here's how it changes when the *benefit* is presented *first*.

Rick: 'Who'd like me to give them complete mastery over this subject?'

(All hands shoot up)

Rick: 'Well, I could probably pack in that extra punch

if we wound back lunch by thirty minutes. Who's with me?'

(All hands shoot up)

Note I didn't say cut lunch by thirty minutes. That would appear to be a loss of time. We simply *wound it back*.

These communication tools will not only have us more prepared for recovery, but will help with our own mental survival, especially if we need to spend extended periods in the company of others during future lockdowns.

**Always show the benefit to the other person first.
What *they* want gets you what you want**

What's in it for me?

The word *'fair'* adds weight to the level of agreement as people generally won't feel comfortable taking advantage of others. And you take your benefit at the back end of the sentence or question. Studies have been carried out to try and find the effect of the concept of *fairness*.

We all want to be *'fair'*. We all want to be seen to be *'fair'*.

'Yes, that's only *fair'*, we say.

But what is *'fair'*? Can it really be quantified?

Although the concept of fairness is as old as us humans, author and ex-FBI hostage negotiator Chris Voss explains how it has been used by the FBI to end hostage situations. In his book Never Split the Difference, he explains that *fair* is impossible to define. One of the favorite words of lawyers working under the English Common Law system is *'reasonable'*. A contract may state 'You will make *reasonable* efforts to do *x, y or z.'*

But who can define what is *'reasonable'*?

Likewise, no one can define what is *'fair'*.

Like *reasonable*, what's *fair* and what's *unfair* is entirely subjective. If we all had the same idea of what *fair* meant, no one would park in disabled parking spaces when they're not actually disabled, and Germans wouldn't put their towels on sun loungers the night before.

So *fair* is foggy and mysterious. And the best way to find out what the other person thinks is *fair* is to *ask them. Not tell them.*

'Would it be *fair?*'

'Let's be *fair.*'

'What's a *fair* price?'

'What do you feel is a *fair* offer?'

You can see that none of these sentences have been *telling* the other person '*take this deal / this price / this blame etc*' but instead are asking them to tell us *what they think is fair.* You'll find that most people's idea of what is fair can be completely different.

'I'd like to pay you to clean my toilets. What do you think might be *fair?*'

The answer will then allow you to make a decision '*yes or no*' — but you keep total control of the negotiation. And even if the answer that comes back isn't totally *fair* (and could be outrageously *unfair*) you can still use *fair* to diffuse and exit the negotiation.

'Ok, that's good to know. Would it be *fair* to ask you if I can take some time to think about it and come back to you?'

'Yes' is the only answer you will get.

Why? Because everyone wants to be *fair*. And it's only *fair* to let them be *fair*, right?

This concept of providing the benefit to the other person

first and your benefit second, along with asking what is *fair*, has proven to be one of the most effective ways to get people in business to give me money.

Anyway, I think it would be *fair* to say I just wish I had learned it sooner!

THE EXTRA PEPPERONI!

- ***Always put the benefit to the other person first in a sentence***
- ***Always frame things in the terms of 'fair' — would that be fair?***

Liar Liar Pants on Fire

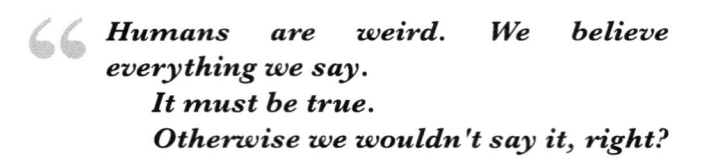

> ***Humans are weird. We believe everything we say.***
> ***It must be true.***
> ***Otherwise we wouldn't say it, right?***

Well, even if we sometimes catch ourselves exaggerating or *guesstimating*, we have an endless ability to justify what *we* say and what *we* hear coming out of *our* own mouths as the gospel truth.

But when others speak, we're not so sure.

'Yeah, I don't know, I'm not sure, could be a scam, what am I being sold here, let me verify this somewhere else.'

We all believe 100% of what *we* say. But as listeners, we actually only believe 5% of what the *other person* says.

. . .

Think of '*Liar liar pants on fire*' as a red flag in other people's Thought Boxes when they don't really believe you.

Which is basically 95% of the time.

The more we go *blah, blah, blah* — the more the others listen with what's called the *inner cynic* and question what we say.

'Really? I don't know about that.'

We therefore need to have most of the words in a conversation come out of the other person's mouth.

What we have to do is say very little, but when necessary ask many questions to get the other person talking. We ask the right questions to get the person we're talking to on our side, but through *their own words*.

Dr Better Make Me Well

If you see the doctor because you have a sore arm, he will probably press it exactly where you told him it was sore. This reinforces the pain, so you'll eagerly take the medicine to make the pain go away.

In other words, you want the solution to the problem as fast as possible and you want it even more so if the pain intensifies. But we all need to believe that Dr Better first *understands* the problem. Which is why he asks us questions. He wants us to tell him *where* it hurts and what it *feels* like. That way we're engaged in the pain and the problem because *we believe 100% of everything we say.*

We provide information by telling. On the other hand, we seek information by asking questions. You won't sell when you try to tell, as people distrust the information you provide. As a result they feel pressured or experience a sense of being sold something. When the others provide the information, they believe 100% in its validity. They won't question or disbelieve it. *The rule here is to always seek information.*

 A funny example to make the point. I could tell my wife why I love her, but a better question according to the science behind 'Liar liar pants on fire' would be: 'So darling, would you tell me why I love you?'

When we explain a process we could tell the other person how the process works. But their inner cynic would be triggered. So instead of trying to bombard them with our facts to convince them that we're right, *we ask a question to get a specific response.*

'Barry, I'd like to buy your widget from you, making monthly payments for a while, then paying you a lump sum down the road sometime.'

Barry replies 'How does that work? Is that legal? I've never heard of that before…'

But how about if I used a pre-loaded question to get Barry to tell *me* how this transaction would work?

'Let me ask you something Barry. Do you know how 'lease to buy' works for something like a car or a TV or a washing machine?'

'Sure Rick. You put a bit of money down, pay something every month and meanwhile you get to use the TV. Then at the end if you decide you want to keep it, you can pay a lump sum off at the end and it's yours.'

'Exactly Barry. If I was thinking of buying your widget the same way, would that present a problem?'

'No, not at all. I guess it's probably fairly easy as people do it with TVs and fridges all the time. I don't know why I hadn't thought of it before, to be honest.'

Barry had just described the process I'd prefer to use to buy his widget, *in his own words*. But I didn't tell Barry how I wanted to do it. I asked Barry a specific question. And Barry told me all about how you can buy a TV on lease terms and that it sounds so easy.

> ## Who just created the terms of this widget sale? Rick or Barry?

The advantage to asking questions is you never tell people anything. Only make observations based on what you've been told from the person you asked.

A way to do this is by starting a sentence with any of these types of phrases:

- *'Have you heard about blah blah blah?'*
- *'Barry said blah blah blah'*
- *'Interesting how some people believe blah blah blah'*
- *'Is there any opportunity in blah blah blah?'*
- *'Would it be fair to say that some people might think blah blah blah?'*

You maintain the trust of the other person by not making any statements of your own. So they have no opportunity for doubt or disbelief.

Because only the *authority* of the information can be seen to be in the firing line, not the *reporter*. In an upcoming book in the series, we'll combine verbal with body language and personal zones.

. . .

Let's now look at some practical ways to get your message and opinion across without *Liar liar pants on fire* or setting off people's negative embedded scripts from the Back Bit of their Thought Boxes.

You can't change what people believe, only get them to question their own beliefs

We can only have them question their own beliefs by asking questions that may lead them to a different conclusion.

For example, sometimes people believe everything they read in a newspaper as the absolute truth, but many people are also able to understand that it's just the media. Therefore you can't tell people what they're reading is trash, they need to see it for themselves.

> **66** *If you don't read the news you're uninformed, if you do you're misinformed*
>
> Mark Twain

What you tell doesn't sell, so ask it this way

When we share our thoughts on a subject, we may find the other person already has a particular viewpoint on it. Asking them to change this can be challenging, but it's possible to do this by *asking them to question their own viewpoint on the subject.*

For example:

Barry: 'I believe Joe Bloggs is the most honourable and credible politician we've ever had.'

Betty: 'Have you always felt that way? Or only since his affair with his secretary went public? Or since he was caught with his hands in the money jar?'

LMAYS - Let Me Ask You Something

As you read this, you're probably noticing the repetition of this phrase '*Let me ask you something*'. But this is very important. When you read it, it's weird, I know. But, I promise, if you use it in daily speech, people *do not notice it*.

They only hear the bit that comes after — *the question*. But by using this phrase — *LMAYS* for short — you focus the listener on the question you're about to ask. *You're asking them for permission to ask a question.* And when someone does that, it's a standard script to comply. *LMAYS acts as a Pattern Break - something we'll talk about later in this book.*

Remember as kids we'd say *'Mom, look at me!'* and she'd be reading the paper and said *'Yes, dear'* without really looking up? But if you'd have said *'Mom, let me ask you something'*, the chances are she'd have put down the paper and asked *'Yes dear, what is it?'*

Her focus would have been on the question instead of the newspaper.

Sometimes when I worry that I'm losing the other person's concentration, I need to have a script that makes me the priority. I do this by simply asking, *'Let me ask you something'*.

Let's say you meet someone new, George. Simply say:

'Excuse me, George. Let me ask you something.'

It doesn't matter how many people are around. George is listening to *you* right now. He will close off all these other sounds to listen to what you're about to ask him. That's because you've just made him the most important person in the room. The LMAYS question defines George as very important, very powerful. And you're asking *permission* for his focus to be on what you say next.

Because the message received by George is *'I'm the guru, the source of all knowledge'* and *'Yes, how can I help you, little person? What is it you'd like to know?'*

The Thought Box cannot concentrate on multiple conversations at the same time. But please don't ever tell my wife that, because when she asks 'Are you listening to me, Rick?', I always tell her I wouldn't miss a word.

Change Their Thoughts & You Change Their Minds

'*Let me ask you something*, Barry — you obviously have a reason for thinking that — do you mind if I ask what it is?'

Then as Barry explains his reasons, he'll start to open up. And sometimes as Barry does this, there's a chance his reasoning will shift while doing it. So if I can get Barry to change it by explaining it to me, I may be able to influence him to reconsider his thought processes and even his prejudices.

In fact, when you ask people to clarify the thinking behind what they believe, sometimes they'll stop, look at you, smile and say *'Actually, it's quite silly when you think about it'*.

And suddenly, we realize that a lot of things that people believe in life don't make much sense when you ask them why they believe the things they do.

Instead of hitting the *Liar liar pants on fire* button and guaranteed resistance by bombarding them with *your* concepts, get into the mindset of the other person as much as you can and get them to explain *their* concepts.

We do that by *asking questions*.

Experiencing Love...of Money!

Has anyone ever tried to offer you payment for something you did and you thought it wasn't enough for all the time and effort that you put in?

That's because everyone has a different idea of monetary value.

So remember that whenever you give people money as compensation, they'll never feel it represents the true value of the service they provided. Instead they'll think you're mean and stingy.

1. ***It will never truly be enough to justify in their mind what they are worth or what they feel they've made or done for you***
2. ***Money is logical with no emotional attachment. It doesn't make people feel anything, so they can't use their imagination to make it bigger***

Instead, *always reward people with an experience*. This lives in their memory forever, along with *who* gave it to them. The perceived value of this experience is almost always far greater than the dollar value.

For example, someone does a good job and you give them an extra $500 on top of $2,000. In their minds, this falls short of what they believe the value of their service to be. On the other hand, being taken up in a hot air balloon for the day is an experience they'll never forget. And the chances are it will have cost you half of what you were intending to give them in cash.

I once gave a number of 42" TVs to some realtors who had helped me throughout that year. They only cost me

$400 each, but came in extra large boxes. I had them delivered to the foyer of the agencies with personal notes addressed to these realtors.

Not only did it create havoc at the agencies, but everybody wanted to know what their colleagues had done to receive these huge TVs. Most people already have a TV but a gift of one, even today, still represents something unusual and surprising.

By the time the word got out and the thank you notes had been opened, I'd already received massive discounts on future property purchases far in excess of what the TVs had cost.

Had I simply handed out $400 cheques, most of the realtors would have thought me miserly and tried to equate what the $400 represented as a percentage value of the work carried out for me throughout the year.

Just suppose I was writing this from the Maldives with beautiful weather all year round, a place people love to visit.

I could tell people *'If you're ever in the Maldives and you want to chill out, you can hang out here. Just empty the garbage on the way out.'*

In reality, most people are pleased to be offered the opportunity but don't even take it up. But they feel as if there's been some Law of Reciprocity at play already, just from hearing the offer. But it provides me with much more financial success to be able to say *'Let me ask you something. If I could organize a vacation for you, all expenses paid, in the Maldives for a week, do you think you could blah blah blah? How would that make you feel?'*

It's hard to put a value on this experience.

Always pay people with an experience, as the emotional element of any experience is hard to value.

Over the years I learned a very interesting human trait which you can also apply to great success in the times ahead.

I've just explained that painting a picture which is then amplified by another person's imagination creates a value in their minds far greater than the physical cost of whatever you're offering.

The reverse of this is best told by telling a story. When I was first starting out I couldn't get people to pay me money as I never studied at university, and therefore in their opinion, I didn't have a certificate to demonstrate my value.

When I tried to quote a fee for a service, people would refuse to pay what I asked. But I discovered that if my fee was *abstract*, then people would actually try to pay me *considerably more*.

How does that make sense? Let's say I walked into a company and suggested I could make their business more profitable if I put it online and removed many of their outdated *standard* processes and embedded costs. When I quoted a fee of say, $5,000, I found that people would argue with me. They'd then try to negotiate with me on *price* alone, not *value*.

The solution turned out to be relatively simple. I suggested that when I had made the changes, my fee would be the first $25,000 of all *newly created profits*, or a fixed % of all the profits going forward.

Switching from a physically defined number - $5,000 in

this case which created friction - moved almost everybody to a position where they believed they would be paying me from future profits. As we know, future profits is a vague concept, very different from $5,000 coming out of the company's bank account today. Because, just like you in your specialism, I have faith in my ability to do a good job. I know for instance how to remove costs and increase profit in a small business that doesn't involve laying off staff. That's a very attractive proposition when the owner doesn't have to pay me today, and then only when I deliver results. By reframing this away from a fixed number towards a concept of future profits, I can charge five times the amount of a standard upfront fee.

We all have skills, and any type of future equity position paid in any form apart from cash upfront is a great way to have others give you more money, especially during difficult times such as now.

Once you have one success of this type of reframing under your belt, no matter how small, other opportunities will appear. The resulting thinking shifts you into accessing other resources from the Front Bit of your Thought Box. And when sharing a Front Bit idea, you transmit it to others around you. They then build and add to your idea. And the group becomes more excited by the rush of endorphins, dopamine and serotonin. This is why we bounce ideas off each other.

SIX

The Question is The Answer

HOW WE PROFIT FROM GIVING, NOT TAKING

When we drive a stick shift car, we cannot simply throw the shifter anywhere we want. Not only will we not move in our desired direction, but we'll also damage the vehicle we're using to get there.

It's the same with communication. It needs to be structured and have a predefined order. If this order isn't followed, the result is damage to the vehicle — which in this case is you.

Whether it's talking to someone you've just met, your kids, your partner or negotiating a business proposal, having a set structure to a conversation will always achieve a better outcome than words randomly coming out of your mouth.

So what does a conversation set structure look like?

When we have a conversation we're selling our point of view, ourselves or a product. Just imagine we had an instruction manual that made our words appear in a certain order so that the other person bought what we were selling nearly every time. Wouldn't that improve our love life or our chances of promotion? You'd be at your best for your date, your boss and all those people wanting to give you money.

So the basics of the art of good conversation is to *say little, use leading questions, and allow others to fill in the blanks.* All of these components will depend on you knowing one very important thing. Knowing where you want the conversation to go - *the outcome.*

Ask leading questions to get the desired outcome

Remember *Liar liar pants on fire* — 95% of everything I say you'll question, while 100% trusting everything everything that comes out of your own mouth, even if it's from embedded thoughts.

So what can we do to avoid raising mistrust in the other person? *We can ask questions*. And it's *the structure of how the questions are asked* that makes a huge difference.

Think of a large plastic funnel which can be used many times in any conversation.

The wide part of the funnel captures answers to a big wide question which can generate multiple answers. It's a question that asks people their opinions on an idea or subject.

The next question is from the middle of the funnel, limiting the answers people can give so the funnel gets narrower.

The final question is asked at the tight end of the funnel, pointing the answer to where you would like it to go.

1. what are your thoughts about lunch?

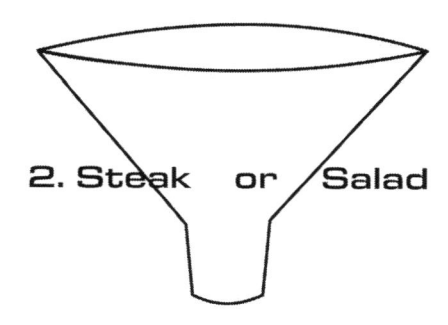

2. Steak   or Salad

3. I think
we should eat
healthy don't you?

1. Big Wide Open Questions
2. Direct or Choice Questions
3. Closed or Tie Down Questions

1. Big Wide Open Questions

Big wide open questions allow us to engage in a non-threatening conversation, giving us an insight into a person's viewpoint on any subject for as long as they want. The questions can be coupled with a little head nodding and the occasional affirmation - *'really?'*, *'wow, that's interesting!'*.

- *'How do you feel about football?'*
- *'How do you feel about Portugal?'*
- *'How do you feel about the weather?'*

- *'How do you feel about the economy?'*

These questions will generate all sorts of answers and information which we can capture with our big funnel.

We've started the conversation with absolutely no idea of where it may go. But the answers, in both words and tone, will give us a huge amount of information about the other person's thoughts, opinions and even state of mind.

With the answers and clues to this first question, we can proceed to narrow it down using the second type of question.

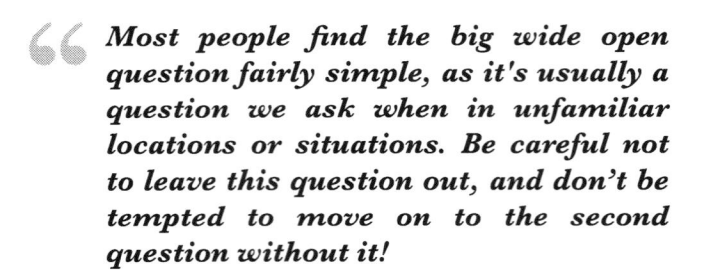 *Most people find the big wide open question fairly simple, as it's usually a question we ask when in unfamiliar locations or situations. Be careful not to leave this question out, and don't be tempted to move on to the second question without it!*

2. Direct or Choice Questions

Our second question, which is the direct or choice question, is designed to filter out the available options and give more specific direction to the topic.

So if our first question was about traveling, we can now better define the topic by narrowing it down to weather and destinations using choice questions.

Q: 'Do you prefer the weather in Lisbon — where it's really sunny - or do you prefer a cloudier place so you don't get so sunburnt — like London?'

> **A: 'I have the type of skin that never burns, so I'd have to say Lisbon, although I've never been.'**

The answer limits the scope of the conversation.

A direct or choice question asked without a preceding open question could easily make false assumptions and alienate the other person.

Just suppose I want to narrow down the routes I'd like delegates to use in order to attend my meeting. I can do this using a choice question such as: *'When you come over, will you come via Jones or Smith Street?'*. I can also achieve the same result by simple statements such as:

- **'Smith St has just been upgraded.'**
- **'I would have planned to use Smith St to come to the meeting.'**
- **'The other guests tend to come via Smith St.'**

Even if there are six ways to get to the meeting, the choice or direct question has limited the options for the other person.

3. Closed or Tie Down Questions

We're now at the tight end of our funnel, and in a position where we can control the direction of the final flow. A closed or a tie down question is designed to predetermine agreement. So we ask it in such a way that it requires agreement - either *yes* or *no* depending on the setup.

A simple example would be:

'An all expenses paid trip to Portugal would probably sound pretty good right now, wouldn't it?'

. . .

Closed questions are often the type of questions you can use to put words in people's mouths:

- *'Little Chris, you'd like an ice cream, wouldn't you?'*
- *'Mom, as long as our homework's done we could watch Cartoon Network, couldn't we?'*
- *'If we meet all the government criteria, it should pass the smell test, shouldn't it?'*

At the basic level, it can be any question assuming agreement ending with

- *'wouldn't'*
- *'couldn't'*
- *'shouldn't'*

But we can go a little deeper.

As we've seen many times already, our Thought Boxes have a tendency to default to 'no'. So here we could actually ask some questions which ask for a 'yes' but disguised as a 'no':

- *'If I helped with the dishes then went out, would that present a problem?'*
- *'If I dropped Little Chris off first and then dropped you off second, would that present a problem?'*

We also have '**No Choice**' choice questions. They appear to be choice questions, but their structure makes them closed or tie down questions.

For example:

'Barry, you're basically a smart man aren't you?'

Barry has a choice but not even he is going to say 'no' to such a loaded question.

Or our old friend *fair*.

'Would it be fair to say that you're a pretty smart person?'

Although we can frame questions implying the other person has a choice, there really is no choice.

Choice question answered when you're like Barry

Choice question answered when you're a *master!*

All Roads Lead to Rome

Let's imagine that Betty's decided the family are going on vacation. She's done plenty of research and has settled on Italy. She only has one problem, convincing Barry.

If you've read this far, you know that Betty has choices with the questions she asks. She could come in straight away like a bull in a china store and tell Barry she's already made the decision.

But what do you think Barry's response would be when Betty says:

'Barry, we haven't been on vacation for ages. Let's go to Italy next month.'

What do you think Barry's going to say?

'Yeah, but I can't really spare the time right now, Betty.'

So if Betty really wants to get Barry to Italy, she'll start using the conversation set structure by asking the *three questions*.

1. Big Wide Open Question:

'Barry, how do you feel about vacations?'

'Oh, you know I love vacations Betty, but I just don't have time right now.'

Okay. Now watch what Betty does with the second question.

2. Direct or Choice Question:

'I know you don't have time, but just suppose we ever

did go on vacation. Would you prefer to have a vacation here or abroad?'

'Well, I don't really have time, but if we were to go somewhere I'd definitely prefer going abroad.'

3. Closed or Tie Down Question:

'And if we ever did go abroad on vacation, it would make sense not to go too far from home in case you needed to get back for work, wouldn't it?'

'Yes, sure. That makes sense Betty.'

'So with that in mind, if we went abroad we'd need to find destinations that were within, say, a couple of hours because of work. I mean, that makes sense, doesn't it?'

'Yes, it does.'

Now Betty has established that Barry likes vacations. He likes them overseas. And he likes them close to home so that he can get back to work if necessary. At each stage, she asked for confirmation from him to make sure her thinking was on track.

Notice also that Betty used the words *just suppose* to introduce an idea that Barry can now think was his own, rather than being *told* what to do. Using *just suppose* is a great way to introduce an idea, process or system without it appearing threatening to the other person. From now on, try starting conversations with *'Hey, I've got an idea'* or *just suppose'* or *'imagine'*.

Now Betty knows that men in particular love to provide *direction* and solve problems.

So later she says:

'Barry, I need your help. I've found that there are only two places that fit your vacation requirements...'

Were they ever Barry's requirements in the first place? Not at all!

'One is Greece and the other is Italy. I need you to pick *one*.'

Betty's biggest concern right now is the choice Barry will make, which once again is the second question. It won't be Mexico. It won't be Brazil. Because she's only given Barry the choice of two. Greece or Italy.

Betty actually wants to go to Italy. She's done the right thing so far to get Barry on board. She started with the big broad question of *'how do you feel about vacations?'* and got him to agree that the destination has to be within a two hour flight.

If she says to him:

'Barry, which one would you prefer? You can choose.'

The choices are Greece or Italy. But she still has one problem. She has left the final choice to Barry and he could end up choosing the *wrong* one. So she has to *weight* her words to make sure he picks Italy.

'We could go to Italy where the food is amazing, or Greece where they had that massive crisis.'

Now we're exaggerating a bit here, but you can see how this works, right?

'Greece sounds a bit suspect, Betty.'

'You're right Barry, that makes sense. Italy it is.'

Betty is now going to Italy. And just to lock it down and close it out, she'll say:

'Barry, because you're so busy, if I just go ahead and book everything, would that present a problem?'

And Barry will say — what?

'No, go ahead, thanks love.'

Next day when Barry goes to work he'll tell his colleagues he's going to Italy. They'll ask him *'when did you decide to go to Italy?'* and he'll say *'Not too sure, actually. It just sort of happened.'*

An innocent conversation was carefully structured to achieve a desired outcome.

The skill is knowing the right questions to ask. To recap, there are three types of questions to ask in this order — *big wide open questions, direct or choice questions* and then *closed or tie down questions*.

Framing the Questions for Maximum Returns

If we're going to ask people questions using the three question conversation set structure, how do we do this without seeming to interrogate them?

If we're not used to asking people questions, someone's bound to respond with:

'Why are you asking me so many questions?'
'Why is this relevant?'
'Why does it really matter?'

So we have to ask permission to ask questions. And in order for us to do this, we need to set up an association where the other person is comfortable with us asking many questions.

 Like everything else in this book, it comes down to the *framing*.

When you go to the doctor, who has the problem, you or the doctor? *You* do. So you naturally assume the position of the person who has the problem that needs fixing. And who naturally holds the solution? The doctor. So by using the doctor set up we establish *who* has the problem, *who* has the solution and *who* will be taking the prescription to feel better.

 The doctor framing is a powerful analogy and set up that I often use

when being introduced to a situation for the first time.

 The doctor's here to help. The doctor has the solution.

As we mentioned earlier when we introduced Doctor Better, Barry's not going to feel like enough attention has been given to his pain. Doctor Better may know what Barry needs, but he must first associate the medicine with the pain, otherwise Barry will not take the medicine. When he squeezes Barry's arm and says *'tell me when it hurts'*, he is reinforcing Barry's pain so that when he gives him the medicine, his Thought Box regards it as the solution to his pain.

THE EXTRA PEPPERONI!

- *Whoever asks the questions controls the conversation*
- *Ask permission to ask your questions ('just like the doctor', 'LMAYS' etc)*
- *Start all conversations with big wide open questions*
- *People only believe 5% of what you say, but 100% of what they say*

Remember, if people can't see the light at the end of the tunnel, they won't board the train.

We haven't made them *feel* the journey yet. This is why we must address *needs* and *wants*.

Next…

 Gotta have it, wanna have it…

Gotta Have It, Wanna Have It

A NEED IS A 'WANT' THAT OUR NEIGHBOR ALREADY OWNS

 Everything we do can be broken down into two things.

    Needs and wants.

    Everybody has needs that have to be met.

    And we have wants we'd like to be fulfilled.

Needs can be things such as hunger, shelter or children. These are non-negotiable and have to be addressed. If they're not addressed, it will result in emotional and/or physical pain. And when the pain becomes unbearable, people will act to avoid it.

We all have *wants* or *desires* which give us a reason for being. Passion that moves us forward with the emotional experience of feeling good. We're all in search of happiness and this is our ultimate *want* or *desire*. And the stranger the desired outcome, the more motivated the person can be to move forwards.

We cannot meet someone's needs and expect them to move forwards emotionally or physically. And merely providing an inspiring future is not enough to get someone's ass out of their chair.

Let's suppose that Betty's girlfriend Dorothy is in an abusive relationship. Betty tells Dorothy to leave so that she can have a better life.

Although that may be true, Dorothy will likely stay where she is. Although her *want* and *desire* for a better life could be addressed by leaving, her *needs* won't. Dorothy still needs to feed little Jimmy, pay the bills and work two jobs. So only when her *needs* are also addressed, can she look to a brighter future.

How often do you share ideas with a friend who says 'That's okay for you to say, but I need to *blah blah blah* before I could consider doing anything like that?'

So Dorothy will never do anything unless it addresses both her *needs* and *wants*.

For instance if I just address your *need* and say:

'I'll just look after that (*need*) for you'.

You'll probably give a non-committal answer and say something like: 'Alright, let me think about it'.

Because if I don't connect that *need* with a strong enough *want*, it won't have the outcome I'm looking for.

'I'll look after that (*need*) for you so you can go and travel the world first class and visit the Louvre in Paris."

Now I'm addressing both your *need* and *want*.

And if your *want* and *desire* were to travel the world first class and inspect the great paintings of the Louvre, it now ticks both boxes for you.

People won't move from one position to another unless

they hear in the same sentence the *want* that they'll achieve by having the *need* met.

You can't do something for someone unless they can *see* or *feel* the benefit of what it allows them to do.

So how do we do this?

We ask a number of information gathering questions that automatically uncover *needs* as well as provide information about people's *wants* and *desires*.

Barry calls me to discuss a problem. The questions I'm asking myself to uncover his *need* could include:

- *'What's the problem?'*
- *'What are the issues that need to be addressed?'*
- *'Are they 'now' or 'later' problems?'*
- *'What have you tried so far?'*
- *'How successful has that been?'*
- *'If this problem doesn't get fixed, what's going to be the outcome?'*

These questions tell us the *need*.

Now, in order to uncover *wants* and *desires*, I may ask Barry one or more of the following questions:

- *'Where would you like to see yourself in say, three years?'*
- *'In a perfect world, what would you like to see happen?'*
- *'If I ran into you twelve months from now, what would you say you'd achieved in order to be happy with the outcome?'*

These questions allow people to see themselves and their business in the future and they'll share with you what they want their future to look like. Of course it's likely to be an idealized future, but they'll see it as clearly as if it were in front of them right now.

Once someone thinks about their future, they employ the power of imagination and thought to put themselves there.

As I said at the start of the book, we need to ask ourselves, 'Is where I am now where I want to be?'. We're facing a unique opportunity to reset, restore and rebuild, but on our own terms, not somebody else's.

Not surprisingly, many people from around the world have contacted me over the last couple of months telling me they've lost their jobs and asking for advice on how to find another one.

In this scenario, I ask them a different question:

'Do you want a *job* or a *way to continue* driving your car, keeping the kids at school and not starving to death?'

I ask each person to define in detail what they believe a job would enable them to do and try to get clarity on the outcomes they want.

A good question to ask would be - '*how do we achieve these outcomes?*'

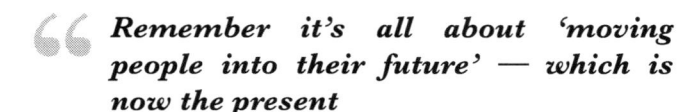 **Remember it's all about 'moving people into their future' — which is now the present**

The more clearly an idea is defined in someone's Front Bit of the Thought Box, the smoother and quicker it will be to take action to achieve it. The more we imagine the perfect vacation — where and when we'll go, where we'll stay, what the weather will be like, what the food will taste like, what we'll see — the more quickly we'll be booking those flights and hotels.

Pattern Breaks

We've seen how we can use questions like *Let me ask you something* - LMAYS - to focus the attention of others. But sometimes we need to bring out the big guns.

If LMAYS is the screwdriver, then the *Pattern Break* is the sledgehammer and any interruption to language flow, speech or thoughts, is known as a *Pattern Break*.

Recently, I made time to see a guy who had flown in from London to meet me in Portugal. As I was answering his questions, he was reading texts on his phone. I would normally have used my standard '*Let me ask you something*' question to grab and focus his attention. But I was too late. The phone had already taken over his Thought Box.

So I picked up a pile of books and dropped them on the floor. The loud bang made him jump in alarm and I said '...and that's why we did it that way' — allowing me to totally re-capture his attention. That was my *Pattern Break*.

The words we use are either influenced by those we

just heard or a thought we just had. If that thought gets scrambled, so do the words that were used to support it.

An example is when someone says 'sorry, I said that without thinking', it's a reaction to what we heard, not what we thought.

Normally, you've actually already scripted out your next few sentences. All language starts with a thought. The sentence structure to communicate that thought is created next, and that comes out of the mouth.

The script process is already embedded and ready to go, no *ummms* required. It's why arguing never gets the other person to change sides. They're not thinking, but simply firing out embedded scripts.

I was having coffee with a friend earlier today, taking a break from writing this chapter. I told her it wasn't necessary for her to say much as her eyes were already telling me her thoughts. She immediately asked 'So what am I thinking then?'. And I knew my answer would open up a barrage of embedded scripts such as:

> *'How do you know?'*
> *'What makes you think that?'*
> *'No I wasn't.'*
> *'Oh, really?'*

So the answer had to be one that didn't spoil the mood.

> **Rick: 'Hey, guess what percentage of people like to be told what they think?'**
> **Friend: 'Zero?'**
> **Rick: 'Yes, I agree... more coffee?'**

People ask me 'How do you speak for hours in front of people without ever being nervous or using the word *ummm* every few seconds?'

The answer is to only ever speak about what you know. If I had to talk about space travel there would be so many *ummms* it would turn into a singalong.

It's like your computer. The cache remembers information to quickly take you where you want to go based on your previous destinations. We remove the embedded scripts or delete the cache using a *Pattern Break*. Your thought process is interrupted and therefore vulnerable to being taken in a different direction using a modified script.

The most common *Pattern Breaks* are caused by our smartphones. Ringtones, notifications and the dreaded WhatsApp whistle. You can see the other person reaching for their phone to check. And when they do that, they're no longer listening to what you're saying. Even when they appear not to react when their phone goes off, often they will say 'Sorry let me turn that off. Now, where were we?'

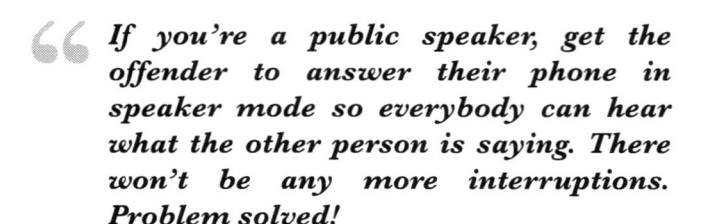

> *If you're a public speaker, get the offender to answer their phone in speaker mode so everybody can hear what the other person is saying. There won't be any more interruptions. Problem solved!*

Just suppose you're having an argument with your partner. You have opposing points of view. And simply arguing never gets the other person to change their point of view. It just makes you both dig in deeper for more embedded scripts to support your point of view.

Your partner says:

'You're a useless messy pig. You never do anything around the house and I don't know why I ever married you.' (*Hmmm, that sounds familiar*).

If you continue arguing, she'll simply find more embedded scripts from the Back Bit of her Thought Box to support her point of view.

Far better to diffuse the argument entirely with a *Pattern Break*.

'Wow look at that mouse!!!'

Your partner's sole focus will be diverted to the mouse in the house. And by the time she's recovered from the shock, she'll have forgotten what the argument was about, as her thought pattern will have been scrambled by your *Pattern Break*.

'Now, what was I saying?'

And just to be a devil, you could reply:

'You were asking if you'd like me to cook you breakfast?'

'Oh, ummm yes of course, thanks.'

The more outrageous the *Pattern Break* is, the more effective.

One of my favorites is:

'Hey, my baby just fell off the shelf!'

Or when I'm on a call and I want to end it politely, I might say:

'Hey, I gotta go, the salt just ran out!'

In a business meeting that you feel is going nowhere, you can create a *Pattern Break* which makes the other side say

'Now where were we?'. This then gives you the opportunity to suggest that it's been a long day and that you should reschedule another meeting. The conversation is now about scheduling meetings, not the actual issue that caused contention.

 Pattern Breaks removes embedded or pre-programmed scripts, allowing you to introduce new ideas that pivot or take the conversation in another direction.

One of the best places to see *Pattern Breaks* at work is in *The Three Stooges* comedies. Check them out on YouTube. You'll see every time one of the Stooges wants to say or do something serious, one of the others creates a *Pattern Break*. The entire humour of The Stooges is based around the chaos caused by *Pattern Breaks*, especially with authority figures who are totally befuddled by their usage.

Next time you receive one of those nuisance calls asking if you've had an accident or a scammer pretending to be your bank, try putting on a broad Australian accent and say:

'That's all very well, but I'd like to talk to you about Jesus.'
They'll surely hang up in seconds.

THE EXTRA PEPPERONI

- **People think first, then speak**
- **Any interruption to language flow is a *Pattern Break***
- **Create a *Pattern Break*, then introduce a modified or changed idea**

Now where was I, (again)?

SEVEN

Sure You Pick... But I Choose

HOW TO WEIGHT YOUR WORDS TO INFLUENCE THE OUTCOME

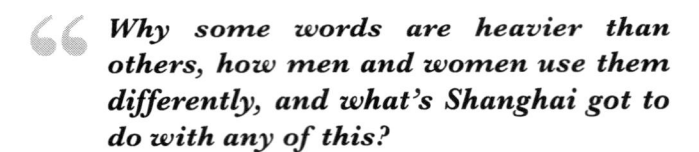 ***Why some words are heavier than others, how men and women use them differently, and what's Shanghai got to do with any of this?***

So far we've looked at some embedded thoughts and responses all of us have, how to choose our words and ask the right questions to get us where we want in a conversation.

We're now going to talk about *Weighted Words* and *Shanghai Words*.

Let me explain.

Some words are *heavier* than others, and we can *weight* those words when we speak in order to influence how we want people to respond. This allows us to take people in a direction they're happy to go. If the conversation were a boat, by weighting the words we lean the direction a little to the left or to the right when it suits us. And as long as nobody falls out of the boat, nobody gets wet.

Sound confusing? Let's start with an example:

. . .

Betty: 'Little Christopher Mumbles! Get off that beach now and into this car at once.'

Betty's frustration sounds like a regular Mom doing a regular Mom thing after a day on the beach.

But what if Betty said: 'Little Chris, do you want to jump into the car right now and have an ice cream? Or would you rather stay on the beach and then come home tomorrow with a stranger?'

We're now getting into *Weighted Words*.

Little Chris: 'Yeah, ice cream.'

What did he also just say yes to?

He also said yes to getting in the car right now.

Weighted Words

We've now seen how we can *weight words* that help lean the conversation a certain way. Start listening to how people phrase their questions to you and how they weight their words to subconsciously influence you in the decisions you make.

Let's look at another example:

Barry: 'Let me ask you something, Betty. There are two places we can go eat. There's the pizza place up the hill, or that place around the corner where the smart people hang out. Which one would you like to go to?'

Which one is Betty likely to pick? It's quite possible she didn't consciously hear the words *'hill'* or *'smart'*, which made the first choice appear less desirable than the second. And if you asked Betty 'Why did you pick that one?', she'll say it seemed easier and sounded better.

Betty could say to Barry, 'I could cook or we can go out.' On the surface it's a choice, right?

Betty's also smart enough to know that if she asks Barry while he's lying on the couch watching the game, she probably isn't going to get her answer. She has no choice but to *weight* the words in order for him to decide to get off the couch.

'I could try cooking for you which I'm more than happy to do. Or we could pop down the road where there's less chance of getting food poisoning. But you decide.'

Now, what can Barry say? What choice does he really have? He's the one being asked to make the choice so he can't say he was manipulated. If Barry picks going out it will be for health reasons. So he'll make the decision to eat out.

Then they might be getting ready to leave the house, and the conversation with Betty undoubtedly goes like this:

'Barry, do you know what you're going to wear? You can't look like you just crawled out of bed.'

'I'm sure I can find something suitable in my closet, but thank you!'

'You could wear that green shirt or there's always that blue one that my girlfriends think you look sexy in. But you pick whichever one you like. It makes no difference to me.'

What's Betty done? She's weighted the words in favor of the shirt that she wants Barry to wear. So which shirt do you think he'll pick?

If she had said 'We're going out tonight and I need you to wear the blue shirt', what do you think Barry might have said?

'Don't tell me what to do! I'll wear any shirt I want, thank you very much.'

But by the time they walk out, Barry will be wearing

the blue shirt and as far as he's concerned, it was his decision all along.

Men do the same but a little different

Business people value their personal time, so if a meeting runs over I might *weight* my words and say:

'This meeting may run over a little if we want to get to our final result. So who agrees with me that it's probably smarter to knock it out today? Alternatively we could find some time over the weekend to meet up if that suits most people.'

What option do you think people will choose?

Next time you're in a job interview, you could weight the words like this:

'Are you looking for someone to work 9-5 or someone who has the flexibility to work late when necessary?'

When you weight the words, your potential employer can see the benefit to hiring you over someone else - not by what you said but by what you asked.

Good businesses employ people mostly based on attitude - and then teach skills to people with good attitudes, not the other way around - so if you're not employed on the spot then you're definitely on the shortlist.

We could flip it around so you're the employer asking the potential employee.

'So Sue, if you were me would you prefer to employ someone who can work 9 to 5 or someone who has the flexibility to work late when necessary?'

THE EXTRA PEPPERONI

- ***Weighted words can make one option***

appear easier or more appealing than the other
- *People usually do not hear the weighted words*
- *Women use them more than men*
- *Best used with the number 2 choice question — 'would you like to do hard x or easy y?'*

Shanghai Words

WORDS THAT CAN TRIP US UP

Has anyone ever said something to you that ended up being opposite of what they meant or how they behaved? The real meaning behind words is often hidden behind what we think they mean.

When Nothing Means *Something*

Language experts call this *meta language*, which is a fancy way of saying *words that hijack the real meaning*.

It sounds as if the words used means one thing, but really the person means something totally different. It's like the words have been *'Shanghai'd'*. For that reason I call them *Shanghai Words*.

Shanghai Words and how they hold you hostage.

In the old days, England's Royal Navy was made up mainly of forced labor. If you got drunk at a port, you could wake up to find you'd been tied up and forced onto a ship to be a sailor for the next five years. You'd just got yourself *Shanghai'd*.

I like to use this term to describe words that can give you one meaning but can actually hold you to ransom and force you onto a ship.

We use them to be socially polite and to hide our true feelings.

People say one thing when they really mean another

Everyone uses *Shanghai Words* but the British are famous for theirs. When an American says 'awesome', they usually mean something is actually awesome. When a Brit says 'awesome', they're usually being sarcastic and mean the exact opposite.

Here's an example of two people bumping into each other. In this case, me and my mate Barry:

'Hey Rick? Is that you mate?'

'Holy shit, is that really you, Barry?'

'God, I haven't seen you in years.'

'Yeah, must be twenty at least.'

'I can't believe it, it's so good to see you.'

'Great to see you too. Look, *we must catch up for a drink sometime.*'

'Yes we must!'

Does this conversation sound familiar? Think about it. I've managed to avoid Barry for the last 20 years. So when I tell Barry, *'We must catch up for a drink sometime'*, what am I really telling him? Even though I've avoided him all that time, I'm still a human being and won't say *'Oh shit Barry, I really wish you hadn't spotted me.'*

So I used *Shanghai Words* to say one thing but mean another. Now Barry probably didn't even notice. He just heard the phrase I wanted him to hear.

So we all use certain words, but we really mean something else. Some are universal and the same in every language and culture. You don't even need to speak the same language to see this going on.

An example of this is when Barry comes home and Betty meets him at the front door. Her mouth looks like she's just finishing sucking a half ripe lemon and both arms and legs are crossed.

He asks:

'What's wrong, darling?'

'*Nothing.*'

We all know that *nothing* means *something*. And if Barry doesn't attend to this or pay attention right away, Betty will now up the ante by banging stuff around the house to let him know this conversation isn't over.

So once again Barry asks:

'What's wrong?'

'Nothing.'

'How was your day then love?'

'*Fine.*' (which means *bad*, right?)

'Look babe, if you won't tell me what's wrong how am I meant to help?'

'Well, if you really loved me you'd *know* what's wrong.'

We've probably all heard and experienced conversations like this.

I have a friend with whom I regularly have conversations like this:

'Hey, you want something to eat?'

'What are you going to cook?'

'I'm going to make some eggs.'

'No I'm alright, you go ahead.'

But in fact he does want to eat. So in a couple of minutes he'll ask:

'You adding fresh parsley?'

(Which means *I hope you understood that when I said 'No, you go ahead' I actually meant 'make double and include me'.*)

Then when I've finished cooking the eggs he'll say:

'Mmm, those eggs smell good.'

(This means *'Can I have some?'*)

'Are you sure you don't want some?'

'I'll just try a little bit.'

(Which means *'Gimme half.'*)

As I spent my years studying the science of these types of word play, I soon came to realize that *'I'm not sure'* means *'talk me into it'*. And sometimes *'always'* means *'never'* and *'never'* means *'always'*.

 'That's interesting' means 'I'm bored by it'

'I'm going to look into it' means 'I'm going to do nothing'

'To be quite honest with you' means they've been lying up to now. And someone using 'but' in a sentence

> ***disbelieves everything they said before the 'but'***
>
> ***'I'd really love to go out with you but I'm busy studying for exams' — means they don't want to go out with you.***

And in business, quite often *no* means *maybe* and *maybe* means *yes*.

We use *Shanghai Words* to work our way through social situations and we can use them to our advantage when we hear them, if we can identify what's going on.

If I present a business proposal and I'm told it's *interesting*, that means they don't like it. If I ask them which part was the most interesting, they'll tell me they found the entire proposal interesting, which is the standard embedded script response.

This response doesn't help me seal the deal. A better question would be to ask which part they found the *least interesting*, as asking this defines the part that they either hated or found the most boring!

Once you learn to recognize *Shanghai Words*, you can have

so much fun responding outside the standard embedded script responses and create your own script.

Where to find Shanghai Words.

It's pretty safe to say that this style of language is used more by women than men.

Biologically, men are programmed only to talk to solve a problem or give direction. Whereas women talk to bond and build connections.

This is why quite often when women say '*talk to me*' they're really saying '*let's connect*'. Whereas a guy is thinking, '*talk about what? I can't find a problem to solve*'. Women are also generally more concerned about personal safety and are therefore less likely to be as direct in conversation as men.

Now let's have a look at how women talk to men and the *Shanghai Words* used. If we listen to women talk, they're more veiled in terms of the true meaning of their conversation. You need to dig down to find out what's really being said, whereas men are usually much more direct.

Women bond through talking

Men can find it frustrating when they can't understand women's use of *Shanghai Words*.

Barry may mention to Betty that he's going out for pizza and beer to watch the game with the boys. She'll say:

'Yeah sure, have a great time. By the way, we're nearly out of milk. So if you're passing the stores on the way home, could you pop in and get some milk? But *don't worry*, it's not that important.' (Shanghai Words for: it's *very* important).

So Barry thinks he's doing fine as Betty has given him permission to go out with the boys.

But when he returns home, the first thing she'll ask is:

Betty: 'Hi darling, did you have a good night with the boys?'

Barry: 'Yup.'

Betty: 'Did you get the milk?'

Barry: 'Well, the store on Smith St looked closed and it's not easy to park there. Besides, you said it wasn't important.'

Betty: 'So you get to go out for pizza and watch the game with your buddies? But when I ask you to do one small thing, you couldn't even go five minutes out of your way to get the milk? Sometimes I wonder why I ever married you, Barry Mumbles!'

And all this time, Barry's thinking 'What did *I* do?'

With *Shanghai Words*, watch for the *downplay*. And it's usually the most important part that is downplayed to hide its importance.

Examples:

'So what have you been up to?' — *Are you seeing someone?*

'Have you been seeing somebody else since me? Not that I care.' — *I care a lot*

'You don't need to answer that if you don't want to.' — *You'd better answer me now!*

'It's not that important.' — *It's very important*

'I'm not really interested.' — *I'm so interested it's keeping me up at night*

'Not that it's any of my business.' — *You'd better bloody tell me*

'Well I'm sure she's pretty.' — *She'd better not be prettier than me*

One of the key ways we move from being a stranger to being a friend is by sharing the same opinion on something. What happens to the relationship is that we now have something in common. Where we were once strangers we now start to come closer together.

Now if I start talking to Barry and we share similar opinions, he'll think:

'You know what, I have so much in common with Rick. I thought when we started chatting that we'd have nothing in common, but in actual fact I'm really enjoying his company.'

Always ask their opinion before you express yours

I Spy With My Little Eye

Hopefully everything you've read up to now will help you develop trust, build rapport and harness support for other areas in your life. Let's now look at *verbal observation*. This enables us to communicate in a style that avoids people feeling anxious or questioned, while at the same time persuading them to give you what you want.

For example, you're at Betty's house and you're dying for a hot drink, but she doesn't ask you if you want one.

You could just say: *'Betty, could I have a cup of coffee?'*, but for most of us that would seem too direct in someone else's house — especially if it's someone we don't know very well.

A better way might be: *'Is that a new Nespresso machine?'* or as an observation: *'Wow, you've got one of those really cool Nespresso machines!'*

Betty: *'Yeah we just got it. Would you like a coffee?'*

 I was at a friend's home and he was cooking dinner. He poured me some pinot noir which I finished rather quickly. I wanted another glass but not wanting to appear greedy, I made an off the cuff remark:

'Wow, this is a good pinot noir that you bought'.

Without turning his head from his cooking, he said 'well, there's another bottle here if you want it'.

It's not that you haven't, you just haven't - *yet*

The point with *verbal observation* is to make people feel proud and noticed through your observation. Then they'll want to share with you because you've paid special attention.

If you asked 'How did you get those front row tickets to the concert?', the response might be 'well I really can't tell you', which is the polite version of the embedded script response and *Shanghai Words* for *'none of your damn business'*.

The *verbal observation* version of it could be:

'OMG! Front row tickets!'. Now the other person feels proud and may well reply:

'Actually they're promotional seats. They often keep the first couple of rows empty for special concert guests who never usually use them. So I always go to the concert 30 minutes before and ask specifically for the unsold promotion tickets. But *shhh* don't tell anyone.'

One great *verbal observation* technique to get someone to share information about almost anything that they've done is to say 'that looks hard!'. You can now pull up a chair while people share with you their entire knowledge on that subject.

Another language accent is the repeating of the last three words of a sentence said by the other person. This is also called *'mirroring'*.

For example, I was recently staying at a buddy's house and one morning I was starving. If I'd gone into the kitchen to make something myself, I would have been in trouble as this is the territory *'owned'* by his wife. She would now arrive to protect it and feel socially compelled to offer to make me breakfast.

Every home has personal territories and domains

Instead, the better move was to wait for my buddy to enter the kitchen. He said 'Morning Rick, it seems a bit *late for breakfast*', to which I repeated '*late for breakfast?*'. He then answered '*well I guess it's not that late, would you like me to cook you some?*'. What do you think I said?

Using the technique of repeating the last three words can be the easier way than asking somebody to make you breakfast. *When we apply the last three words, we implant a thought in the other person.*

Let Me Make It Easy For You — The Rule of Association

Another way of getting someone to accept a solution is to get them to associate it with something familiar, and describe a simple and normal process to them, by way of *association*.

When people ask '*How does something work?*', we tend to explain an unfamiliar process to them by default. When we do that they end up thinking, 'I've never heard of this before, so let me think about it'. This means they're questioning the validity of what we're saying, and could easily think it's a scam or even illegal.

So here's an example of how to present something unfamiliar, but still get it accepted. This is a good way to present your idea by creating *association* and avoiding *Liar liar pants on fire* with you trying to *sell* people your idea, your concept or your widget.

This example allows the other person to buy into the concept and *own* the outcome.

Barry: 'Hey Rick, how much is the widget?'

Rick: 'It's $400,000 if you'd like to buy it. And you can make payments directly to me.'

Barry: 'Really I've never heard of that. So how does that work?'

Rick: 'Let me explain. Do you know how a bank loan works?'

Barry: 'Yeah.'

Rick: 'OK Barry, can you talk me through that process then?'

Barry: 'You get the money from the bank. And you make monthly payments to pay it off. Or if you want you can sell the widget, take the profit and pay out the bank. In the meantime, the widget is yours.'

Rick: 'So this is the same Barry, but instead of the bank, you just pay me directly. Does that sound like something that would interest you?'

Barry: 'Sounds pretty good to me. How long does it take?'

Rick: 'Have you got seven minutes, Barry?'

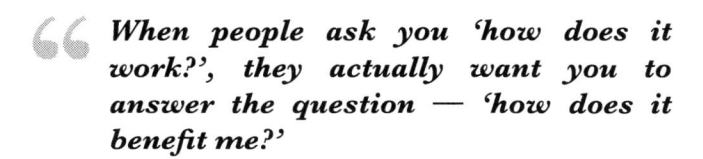

> **When people ask you 'how does it work?', they actually want you to answer the question — 'how does it benefit me?'**

Associations and *analogies* create that *aha* moment for understanding.

As a smart communicator, you should always have your analogies ready for the situation at hand. Think of the best and easiest way to get the other person to consider your proposal.

Once someone aligns themselves with an *analogy* that you've given them, they'll start to align themselves with you, the person giving the analogy.

A good analogy structure will get the other person to understand a point being made or a process being explained, without having any previous experience or knowledge about it.

Using an analogy relating to someone's work, hobbies or sporting interests makes it easier for people to understand you, as well as accepting it as being *normal, standard* and *legal*. When I meet new people, I make a point to ask about these topics, in case I need to draw on them later.

Most conversations are spent expressing our *points of view*, and it's this point of view that fuels the ongoing banter.

When we combine all the elements we've learned so far, the next step is to have a conversation with a *set direction* and *desired outcome*. And in order to control and manage this process, we need to learn how to *open the gate* and *close the gate*, as we move along each step of the way until we're all on the same page.

THE EXTRA PEPPERONI

- *Actively listen to what the other person's saying*
- *Follow the actions, not the words*
- *Read 'Talk Language' by Allan Pease (it even has a picture of me in it!)*

EIGHT

One Step Negotiation

'Hey Barry, I've got this great idea. Let's get together a group of friends who love fishing and we can put some money in a pot. Then every week we'll fly somewhere to fish. It can be like a club and you can be the President, but you'll have to make sure everyone pays their dues each month and…'

 Wait! Hold up!

It makes you anxious just reading it doesn't it?

While we have many languages, we also have different styles of communication. What I've found works is one where everybody wants to be involved in whatever is happening without being asked. This has certain formulas we're about to learn.

Whether it's wanting others to share your ideas or you wanting a buy a *genuine* $9 Rolex at the Casablanca Casbah — (by the way mine still works).

. . .

Have you ever done any of the following? —

- ***Demanded a raise from your boss because your workload has increased or you simply feel you deserve more compensation?***
- ***Told your kids they have to be in bed by a certain time which then led to arguments and tears before bedtime?***
- ***Sent a business proposal to a potential customer where you outlined everything you and your company could offer, including the price?***

Very often, in fact more often than not, these 'negotiations' fail, but we never find out why. The other side will often use embedded response scripts like —

> ***'Let me think about it.' — which means 'no'.***
> ***'Let me check with my partner/boss' — which means 'no'.***
> ***'I just need to compare it to the other quotes we received' - which means 'no'.***

Not only do we get rejections, which nobody likes, we also don't get any feedback on why our proposal or request failed.

Most people present a proposal all in one go, but then it's hard to dissect and figure out which sections didn't work if the entire proposal is rejected.

For example, when I was much younger, I'd meet girls who said *no* to going out with me, and when I shared my tears with my buddies they'd ask me questions such as:

- ***'Did she say no because she didn't speak English?'***
- ***'Did she say no because you don't have a job?'***
- ***'Did she say no because you think of McDonalds as a three course meal?'***
- ***'Did she say no because you don't like cats?'***
- ***'Did she say no because you asked her mother out first?'***

The problem was I never knew the answer because I'd never been taught the technique of *one step negotiation*.

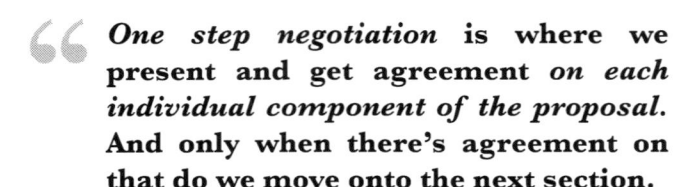

One step negotiation is where we present and get agreement *on each* individual component of the proposal. And only when there's agreement on that do we move onto the next section.

Whether it's an idea you want your partner to take seriously, like moving to Alaska or a business proposal, every negotiation can benefit from a *one step negotiation* approach. This communication technique is far superior to the usual 'present everything and hope for the best' approach.

Closing the Gate

'I heard you might be interested in stocking our furniture?'

'Yes we're looking for some new brands and we're considering yours.'

'Excellent, well our furniture would usually be delivered every Wednesday. How would you feel about that?'

'Yes, that would work.'

'Great. We'd need your order 14 days in advance, in order to pull the stock from the warehouse for delivery. Would that work for you?'

'Mmm, 14 days is a bit too long. We'd prefer 10 days.'

'So if we could agree to modify this section to ordering 10 days before delivery, would that be satisfactory?'

'Yes.'

'Great. Well, for a 10 day stock we currently only do two different types of materials. We do leather in two colors and we have cotton in four colors.'

'Yes, we're happy with those options.'

So what we're doing here is going through each section of our imaginary business agreement. As we do this, we're ticking each box and can address every single issue as it arises.

Otherwise the *standard* approach would be for the salesperson to visit the client, chat about the product, leave a brochure and business terms so the client can '*have a think about it*', then wonder why the client never got back to them or returned a signed contract.

Instead we address the potential issues directly, such as the delivery day. For a large customer it's the kind of issue that could mean the difference between a *yes* and a *no*, but only when we know the specific issue.

One by one, we *open the gate and we close the gate*. Then we have an excellent chance of ending up with an agreement that satisfies everyone.

If you don't negotiate this way and you don't get the

order, the response will be 'sorry, *we decided to go with someone else*'.

A discussion or conversation will either be in your control or out of your control, depending on how you present it. A proposal negotiated *one step* at a time can expose the most common objectives which you can learn from and benefit the business. This kind of information is worth its weight in gold.

One step negotiation with friends

'Hey Betty, do you want to go down to the beach? It's 30 minutes away. We're going via the beach road. My friend has a fishing boat, so we can go out fishing in it.'

Betty says she doesn't want to go. If I ask her why, she'll probably say something like 'I'm not in the mood today,' so as to not hurt my feelings. Perhaps Betty likes the idea of going to the beach, but hates fishing? But how would I know? Giving her the full proposal in one go instead of breaking it down into smaller parts means I'll never know which part of my proposal hit the skids.

A better way to communicate the same idea would be to break it down using *one step negotiation*.

'Betty, we're going to the beach, you wanna come along?'

'Yup.'

'It's 30 minutes away. Are you ok with that?'

'Yup.'

'We might go fishing too.'

'Sounds good to me.'

'My mate has a boat.'

'Well, actually I don't really like boats.'

'OK, well how about we don't go in the boat, but we fish from the shore?'

'Yeah sounds great. I'll grab my stuff!'

By using this *one step negotiation* technique, we discovered that *Betty doesn't like boats.*

Everything comes back to *one step negotiation* and the '*Open the Gate, Close the Gate*' approach. By going through the elements of the conversation one step at a time, you'll know what needs adjusting in order to bring it all together — or at least understand where it falls apart if that's what happens.

THE EXTRA PEPPERONI

- *Every social and business proposal has numerous components, so break them down*
- *Seek agreement on each component INDEPENDENT of the other components*
- *Never move onto the next component unless you've agreed on the previous one*
- *Write in the manner that you speak and leave out sections to get the other side asking questions*

We're nearly at the end of our journey. But we have one more incredible weapon that trumps all the others. It's better than *Weighted Words*, more powerful than *Pineapple Words*. And the good news is it's always in our favor.

The Power of Silence

HOW TO GET WHAT YOU WANT BY SAYING NOTHING

> **Silence is very powerful. That's because by saying nothing you get a lot of people giving you money.**

This could be through considerable discounts or giving you extra goods and services.

An example of this is with text messaging, where no response to a text message or *silence* is understood as the equivalent of saying *no*.

If you send someone a text saying 'Let's go out tomorrow at 6pm' and you don't receive a reply, what's the answer? '*No*'.

In a conversation, silence can push the other person to compromise their position.

There are two reasons for this:

1. They'll take the silence as a sign that what is proposed is

unacceptable. However, you're happy to listen to the other side's offer. Hence the silence.

2. Like most people, they'll struggle with the social awkwardness of being silent. Somebody will need to fill the dead space with words and whoever speaks first will compromise their position.

Stay silent when a car salesperson says *you can have the car for the special price of $30,000'* . Don't be surprised if they offer the car at a lower price in order to end the silence.

'OK, I wouldn't normally do this but on this one occasion, I could do $27,000.'

You stay silent.

'Well you're beating me up here, the best I can do is $25,000. Take it or leave it.'

What did you *actually* say? Nothing. But by saying nothing, the other person just gave you $5,000.

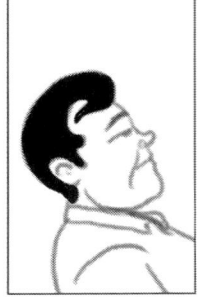

When I'm buying things, my silence usually means a lower price might be offered by the seller. Often the seller will jump in and say 'well the price *is* negotiable' — just to break the awkward silence.

I've been known to sit in silence during a negotiation, listening to the clock ticking in the eerie silence. If nothing comes back, I might say *'ummm'* after a minute or so. Then another *'ummm'*. Eventually I might say *'Is that the best you can do?'*

After some sweaty silence, the response will often be some kind of compromise — either a lower price or better terms.

Staying silent tells people that you're not on board or happy about the current situation. There's no need to use words. Less is more.

Men find it very frustrating when they're presented with silence by women who use this as a tactic to win concessions.

Remember the earlier conversation where Barry comes home and is met with silence?

Barry: 'What's wrong?'

Betty: 'Nothing.' (which is a *Shanghai Word* for *something*)

Barry: 'I know something's wrong, what is it?'

Betty: 'Well, if you loved me you'd know.' (which means *'if you're too dumb to figure it out, I'm not going to tell you.'*)

Barry ignores Betty who starts banging things around the house, which means *'we need to work this out and you need to apologize.'*

Next, Barry will start making promises about his future behaviour and Betty will speak only when she feels they've come to a satisfactory compromise.

Silence is a great tool to use to voice disagreement with what's being offered without using the voice.

THE EXTRA PEPPERONI

- He who speaks first loses
- Less is more
- Use *'Is that the best you can do?'*
- Ask 'so what do I get for free if things don't work out as expected?' as you'll be surprised what people will give away

NINE

'How To' Scripts

WHAT TO SAY, WHEN TO SAY AND HOW TO SAY IT

 ### *How To Talk To Make Sure You Get The Outcome You Want*

When I started to write these scripts for you to learn and use in real life situations a number of my advance readers told me they felt they could never say the words as they were printed on the page. This makes a lot of sense because as you'll soon hear, I have a very distinct way of talking and especially asking questions.

I realized that it's more important that you hear the *tone* of how I ask these questions rather than the words I use — because as you may know, only 7% of communication comes from the actual words we use and 38% from how we *say* those words. A whopping 55% comes from non-verbal communication; the way we stand, the tilt of a head, hand gestures and body language in general.

Free Bonus Material

We all have different ways of speaking, regardless of language or accent. It's important that you feel comfortable with these scripts in the way that you talk to others.

So I decided to put links to some audio clips so that you can hear how I phrase things. You can copy the the words, using your own speech patterns but more importantly copy the *tone* of what I'm saying and how I'm asking the questions.

For all these scripts you need to sound natural. So practice on your friends, using expressions that you'd normally use, but pay attention to how I stress certain words.

You can find the original audio content by clicking below
Bonus content

The scripts include some powerful *Shoehorn Words*, *Weighted Words* and even a few *Pineapple Words* when it's our intention to blow up the conversation for our own purposes. Or just record yourself on your smartphone and rehearse until you sound natural. Then you're pretty much ready to go.

Remember, it's really important to hear the tonality of the scripts and the words that we should be using, so make sure to check out the audio clips and written examples on the website.

 We've only covered scripts for a few examples here although many of the communication patterns are interchangeable. If you have any

scripts you'd like me to help you with free of charge, just ping me on any social media. I'll tell you how to get in touch with your questions and help you create a script for any purpose.

I'll be adding more free and exclusive content for readers over the coming months.

Rick

We've Only Just Begun

So, dear reader, we've now reached the end of the first book.

The takeaways I wanted to share were how to train your Thought Box so your ideas come from the *Front Bit* and not the *Back Bit*.

The next takeaway should be how to alter other people's thought patterns to better match your own, as well as communicate ideas that will be more eagerly accepted by others.

What we've covered are various elements of language patterns which, when applied correctly, can have you communicating in a different and highly effective style. Not only could this boost your popularity, but it could also get you more of what you want. Remember we learned how the subconscious mind thinks it first — then instructs the conscious mind how to act. The journey into subconscious thinking gets other people wanting to get involved with you on some level, without even realizing exactly why. As mentioned earlier, this science isn't something you master overnight. My journey into body language and talk language started as a teenager from humble beginnings before the subject became more mainstream. At the time, there were only various scientific papers available and I read everything I could find. By learning and practicing the crafts throughout my life, I've been able to share some of them with you here.

Moving forward, I would pick just one element to practice, such as *Weighted Words*, and you'll quickly see results. It's like learning a language. Practice on your friends as it doesn't matter if you make a mistake. They'll still be your friends. I'm the world's best goof up guy and I still keep going.

One thing is for sure, the world tomorrow, next week and the months and years ahead are going to look very different indeed. The long talked of New World Order has arrived without anyone actually planning for it. But now we have the instruction manual, right? So we can at least be more prepared than the next person and can therefore reset, restore and rebuild our lives.

P. S. If you're also a little different, be proud of it and accept that some will love it and others won't get it — that's life. All the best...

Rick Otton

You've just finished reading "How to Get People to Give You Money"

www.theupgradedthinking.com

Some Further Reading

Here are just a few of the books you might like to check out that deal with the brain and communication.

Remember to check out the free bonus material at Theupgradedthinking.com/rick-otton-bonus-content/

Daniel Kahneman - Thinking, Fast and Slow
    David Eagle - The Brain
    Chris Voss - Never Split the Difference
    Robert Cialdini - Persuasion
    Robert Cialdini - Pre-suasion
    Allan & Barbara Pease - Talk Language
    Allan & Barbara Pease - Body Language
    Neil Slade - The Frontal Lobes Supercharge

Printed in Great Britain
by Amazon